REDEEMING
THE
CREATION

REDEEMING THE CREATION

The Rio Earth Summit:
Challenges for the Churches

Wesley
Granberg-Michaelson

BOOK SERIES

WCC Publications, Geneva

iv

Cover design: Rob Lucas

Cover photo: World-View

ISBN 2-8254-1091-8

© 1992 WCC Publications, World Council of Churches,
150 route de Ferney, P.O. Box 2100, 1211 Geneva 2, Switzerland

No. 55 in the Risk book series

Printed in Switzerland

Table of Contents

BT
695.5
G714
1992
x

Foreword

Two months ago, during the closing days of the Earth Summit in Rio de Janeiro, I looked around the assembled leaders who had come from all over the planet — more than a hundred heads of state, and thousands of people from virtually all sectors of society — and I had visions of the future. A future where creation will indeed be redeemed.

Together with millions of people I believe that the prospects for our earth cannot, must not, be the same after the Earth Summit elevated the awareness of people and their leaders to the crisis our civilization faces as a result of the damage we are inflicting on our earth's environment and life-support systems in the pursuit of our economic and development goals. Rio altered the environment and development dialogue fundamentally, linking poverty, equity and social justice with the achievement of sustainable development.

We may be accused of striving for the unrealistic, but in this last decade of the 20th century sustainable development must be seen as indispensable to the redemption of our common future.

Ours has been a participatory process. Through their own organizations millions of people have been involved in the tasks of preparing for this largest United Nations conference ever: non-governmental organizations, youth, children, indigenous people and media. They have provided strong answers to our question: "What on earth is to be done?"

For the first time in the history of the United Nations, NGOs played a formal role throughout the preparatory process leading up to Rio and at the Earth Summit itself. One-third of the official government delegations included NGO representatives. The World Council of Churches has been one of the pioneer partners, particularly because of its early commitment to a "Just, Participatory and Sustainable Society". My own past involvement with the World Council and Sodepax made me aware of the deep and longstanding commitment of the churches to these issues. Christian communities around the world have been among those providing building blocks for a better future.

Of course, satisfaction over some of the Earth Summit achievements — Agenda 21, the Rio Declaration, conventions on climate change and biological diversity, to mention a few — cannot let us forget what has not yet been achieved. We cannot ignore the reality that some of our goals have been weakened, that we need stronger commitments on finance, that targets and timetables must be set for conventions to be effective. But overall, Agenda 21 constitutes the most comprehensive and far-reaching programme of action ever approved by the world community. And the fact that this approval was at the highest political level lends it special authority and importance. For the first time in international politics we have consensus that the future of the planet is at stake if we do not reverse the process of abusing it.

The real measure of success will be in what happens now, after Rio, when government leaders and citizens alike have returned to their countries, to their organizations, to their own lives. It is up to all of us to build on the foundations laid by the Earth Summit. The decisions that have been taken at global levels need to be translated into national politics and practices at all levels — down to the smallest unit.

I would urge the churches to take a lead in developing their own version on Agenda 21.

The process of participation has meant much to me during the many years I have tried to work for the future of our planet. After Rio, I believe more than ever that it is only if all sectors of society participate in the political and United Nations organizations processes that a lasting change of political will can be achieved. A new world order, as we move into the 21st century, must unite us all in a global partnership — which always recognizes and respects the transcending sovereignty of nature, of our only one earth.

August 1992   MAURICE F. STRONG
                     Secretary General
                     United Nations Conference
                     on Environment and Development

Introduction:
Christ the Redeemer

The statue of Christ the Redeemer towers high above Rio de Janeiro, with outstretched arms and an expression of pathos and compassion. The statue is the landmark of Rio. Residents of this city of 11 million say they look for it whenever they have lost their way and need directions.

As you stand at the base of this statue, the city, with all its beauty and pain, stretches out before you. Its striking downtown faces out to parks and the sea; its streets are filled with business people, but also are the only home for many of those in Rio — one out of every five residents — who are homeless. To the south Rio's magnificent beaches lie unfurled, rimmed by stony peninsulas and separated by hills and ridges disappearing into the ocean. Behind them are the high-rise hotels and apartments offering luxury to many thousands both from Rio and throughout the world.

Away from the beaches, winding up the hillsides, are the favelas, the shantytowns where the hundreds of thousands of Rio's poor find their homes. Sometimes those communities have water and sewer systems. Often they do not.

Christ the Redeemer also looks out over the smoky, dirty skies to the north, clogged with the soot of industry, and the constant parade of ships slipping through a narrow entrance from the open sea into the wide protected waters of the Bay of Guanabara which provide Rio's harbours. Imports arrive and are unloaded, exports are taken away, and Brazil's foreign debt remains.

From the foot of the statue atop the mountain, the city looks stunning in its beauty, drama and charm. But Christ's look of pathos also sees the violence, anxiety and despair. Homeless children are murdered each day; most are black. Thousands of desperate women try to sell themselves to stay alive. The middle class are afraid to ride buses or ferries wearing their watches and earrings. And many see no clear way to a future with promise.

For fourteen days in June 1992, Rio welcomed the "Earth Summit" into its midst. Nothing quite like this had ever happened before in history. Representatives of 178 nations of the world gathered to consider the prospects for the future of humanity and the sustainability of the planet. Titled the United Nations Conference on Environment and Development (UNCED), the gathering had as its aim the formulation of cooperative international policies to protect the earth and meet the needs of its growing number of inhabitants. At the conclusion, over 100 heads of state came for the most inclusive "summit" meeting of governmental leaders in history. Ninety-two hundred journalists were there to report on the Earth Summit — more journalists than had ever been present at any event.

The Earth Summit included not only government delegations, but also the official presence of an astonishing number of non-governmental organizations (NGOs) — over 1,400 — who were accredited to the conference. But even more, thousands of additional people and representatives of organizations gathered together at the "Global Forum". This festival included participation by representatives from over 7,000 organizations from around the world. Held at Flamengo Park in downtown Rio, as well as at various other meeting sites throughout the city, this gathering featured up to 60 separate meetings, forums and discussions on any given day, addressing various dimensions of planetary survival.

And to the Earth Summit, the churches also sent their representatives. Some church organizations and ecumenical bodies were among the 1,400 officially accredited NGOs at the governmental conference. Others were participants in the Global Forum. Large delegations from the Methodist Church and the United Church of Christ in the USA came to Rio to be part of this gathering. Others came to participate in various interfaith meetings, vigils and events.

The World Council of Churches convened a major ecumenical meeting which was one of the myriad events at the Earth Summit. For the first seven days of June, a group of 176 people from 54 countries and over 70 different churches met in an area on the north side of Rio called Baixada Fluminense. There they reflected, worshipped, discussed, and responded to the issues of the Earth Summit from the perspectives of churches worldwide. And they were embraced in lively fellowship by the Catholic and Protestant churches in this area — a place known as one of the most violent in Brazil, typifying the realities of suffering, social strife and economic despair which mark much of Brazilian life.

So during the first fourteen days of June, the open arms of Christ the Redeemer reached out to all those who had journeyed to Rio with their various dreams, hopes, policies, positions and proposals for redeeming the earth.

When the WCC ecumenical meeting, titled "Searching for the New Heavens and the New Earth: an Ecumenical Response to UNCED" opened, its local host, Catholic Archbishop Dom Mauro Morelli, said that the left arm of Christ the Redeemer was pointing north, towards the gathering in Baixada Fluminense. "If Jesus came to the Earth Summit", he told the group, "he would come here, to where people are suffering, looking for a promised future". And indeed, if you stand beneath that statue of Christ and look to the left along the Bay of Guanabara, you will see the grey dusty horizons to the north, where hundreds of thousands search for justice and life and where representatives from churches around the world came to gather.

Flamengo Park, the site of the Global Forum, is in front of the statue. Under its watchful gaze thousands came to the park each day, some trumpeting the good deeds of their organization, others looking for new wisdom, many just wandering through this festival of ideas and plans for saving the earth. Movie stars, presidents, UN officials and NGO celebrities opened this event. A sailing ship named Gaia, carrying children who started their journey in Scandinavia and travelled to New York,

Washington, the Caribbean, and a thousand kilometres up the Amazon, as ambassadors of the future generation, arrived on the beach of Flamengo Park for the celebration opening the Global Forum.

The government delegations, however, met off to the right and a little behind the statue, at a spacious and modern convention site named Riocentro. Guarded closely by military and police, the centre served as an ideal facility for a high level meeting of thousands from governments, international agencies and NGOs. Yet it was isolated not only from real Brazilian life, but also from downtown Rio and the Global Forum.

The three sites — Baixada Fluminense, Flamengo Park and Riocentro — were like three separate worlds. The geographical distances between them could take an hour and a half to travel. But the emotional, political and spiritual distances separating them were often far more difficult to overcome. And yet, the arms of Christ the Redeemer reached out to encompass each of these three places. Indeed, they reach out, from atop that mountain above Rio, to embrace the whole of the earth, pleading compassionately for its survival, for the fullness of its life.

The Earth Summit offers the world's churches a fresh occasion, in the months and years ahead, to see the pathos of Christ in the midst of creation's contemporary turmoil and destruction and to discern how they can join the outstretched arms of Christ the Redeemer to bring healing and life. Moreover, the Earth Summit calls the churches, and in particular the ecumenical movement, to discover anew their own role amidst these three different worlds present those fourteen days in Rio, and present in societies everywhere. Where, indeed, shall we root our search for "the new heavens and the new earth"? In the life and witness of the churches, living and ministering and holding forth in word and deed God's promises in the midst of where people — and the earth — are suffering? Or is it in the midst of the explosion of groups and movements who are alerting the world to its present peril and organizing, mobilizing and acting on specific issues? And what of those centres of political power and decision-making — the places where laws, agreements, treaties, declarations, and also practical commitments, involving billions of dollars, are actually made?

Ecumenical work around the world faces new questions and challenges because of the Earth Summit. Some of these involve the substance of Christian witness in the world today, in light of new understandings of the global crisis. But others go deeper, involving the style, methods and assumptions which undergird the churches' life and witness.

Thus reflection on the Earth Summit involves far more than appraisals of whether and where this event "succeeded" and "failed", according to its standards. The churches are challenged to look again at the presence of Christ the Redeemer in the midst of the Earth Summit and to discover how his presence can most clearly be expressed for the redeeming of the earth.

1. The Failure of Development

Historically the Earth Summit will come to mark the time when the world realized that development as traditionally understood had failed. When efforts at post-war reconstruction began as the world emerged from the Second World War, hopes began to dawn for economic progress among the whole human family. The nightmare of world war could be replaced, it was hoped, with the dream of building global prosperity and security.

While the emerging Cold War began to vanquish hopes for an era of peace and mutual security, commitments were made to the possibilities of global economic growth and "modernization". President Harry Truman, in his inaugural address of 1949, referred to the "under-developed areas" of the world. And a common goal of "development" for them was defined and set.

Wolfgang Sachs of the Institute for Cultural Studies in Germany, writing from the Earth Summit, put it this way in discussing the roots of the development era: "The degree of civilization in a country could from now on be measured by its level of production. This new concept allowed the thousands of cultures to be separated into the two simple categories of 'developed' and 'under-developed'. Diverse societies were placed on a single progressive track, more or less advancing according to the criteria of production".

All this implied, of course, moving forward towards a single model and goal, which was seen principally in the economy of the United States and other affluent societies of the North. Increased economic production became the key measurement of progress and the sole means for advancing towards this goal. As Truman stated, "greater production is the key to prosperity and peace".

Of course production requires investment. And economic progress requires planning, along with technical tools and skills. This had to be provided by those with wealth and capital. So agencies and organizations — national, international, public and private — were established to channel this flow of aid for development. In the United States, it was the Agency for International Development (USAID), under the State Department. International bodies in conjunction with the United Nations, including the World Bank, carried forth the same mission.

The idea was that the contribution of resources and skills could help start this process of modernization and "development". Funds given first as outright grants could later be combined with concessional loans. A climate would be established in which private banks would also have confidence to participate, providing the capital for investment of corporations in producing goods and developing markets within these societies. The clear assumption was that as these economies began to grow, they would generate the money needed to repay the costs of using this initial capital. And gradually, these economies would become integrated into the global economy, with the benefits increasingly reaching to the whole of their populations.

Many hopes for such "development" in those early years were genuine, idealistic, and often motivated by concerns for global justice. But other, less idealistic motives were also involved. The West increasingly saw development as part of its fight against communism, and not just against poverty. The East as well invested resources in countries where it hoped to gain political influence. Goals became easily mixed, compromised and confused.

And the patterns of aid programmes from northern nations had to be justified to political constituencies. Thus, pay-offs at home had to be shown for aid given abroad. This affected even the most humanitarian of government programmes. By the early 1970s, for instance, the US programme by which the government bought surplus wheat and rice from its farmers and donated it to meet the critical needs of the hungry, had become deeply politicized. Despite widespread hunger and shortfalls in harvests in south Asia and Africa, the US government, pursuing its own political agenda, was giving up to half of this food to allies like South Korea, South Vietnam and Egypt to support their budgets.

Yet the real crisis of development was far deeper. Twenty-five years after the Second World War, even the architects of development were beginning to realize that it was simply not working. True believers pointed to success stories like South Korea and Taiwan. But the list was short, and not growing. Growth itself was not growing.

Even when wealth for some was successfully created, poverty for many more was increasing more rapidly. The "underdeveloped" world was not "catching up" with the developed world. In many respects, the gap between the rich and the poor was growing wider, rather than being narrowed. Massive development projects to build dams, highways, power stations and factories did not eliminate hunger, malnutrition, infant mortality and widespread poverty.

Attempts were made at redefining development on a smaller scale and redirecting it to those most in need. Wide recognition was given to rural populations, small farmers and women. Increasing questions about large-scale development projects and transfers of elaborate industrial technologies were raised by many who began to think, with E.F. Schumacher, that "small is beautiful".

Yet, while one can find smaller "successes" based on these attempted reforms and innovations, the global picture by the time of the Earth Summit was marked by the failure of four decades of development. No one could argue, in the face of brute facts, that the post-war dreams of shared global prosperity were being achieved.

The best that could be said was that a small middle and elite class had been created in the South, whose life-styles, aspirations and careers were tied to the consuming and absorbing societies of the affluent North. But on the whole, this new class was not serving as the means for expanding economic growth to the bulk of their countries' populations. Even their bank accounts were often held in northern countries.

But more than this, by the time of the Earth Summit, a growing number of voices were saying that the whole path of development was headed in a misguided and self-destructive direction. The whole world simply couldn't and shouldn't catch up with the "leaders". The entire paradigm was wrong.

Discussion about the "limits to growth" in the 1970s first introduced these questions. Scientists and other thoughtful observers began to think about what would actually happen if the whole world lived like the first world — and if the whole kept growing. It was a recipe for disaster.

So the entire model of continued economic growth and expansion of affluent economies, spreading its economic life to the "developing" societies, as the means for human liberation, was questioned at its core. The planet simply couldn't sustain this; three or four extra planets with their resources might be required!

In this light, the path of the affluent North was not progress; it was leading, instead, to the rising temperature of the globe's atmosphere, the deterioration of its ozone layer, the poisoning of its waters, the loss of its soil. And these effects, while caused chiefly by the North's consumer economies, were felt globally, and particularly by vulnerable peoples and environments in the South. Further, investment by the North in the South had resulted more in economic bondage than freedom as economies of many countries were crippled under the burden of debt payments.

The underlying assumptions of this model of progress had come under focused and searching criticism by the time of the Earth Summit. Many of these voices were heard on the fringes of the official discussions. Yet, clearly, the framework of understanding was beginning to shift.

One of those voices questioning economic orthodoxy regarding development is Herman Daly. Formerly a professor of economics, his writings focused for years on ideas of a "steady state" economic system. And as a thoughtful Christian, he has attempted to relate theological understandings and ethical values to his economic approaches. With theologian John Cobb, Jr, he co-authored a widely respected book, *Towards the Common Good*. More recently, he became the senior economist in the Environmental Department of the World Bank — a move which surprised many in light of the traditional approach of that institution and his more heretical economic ideas.

Daly came to Rio de Janeiro to address the World Council of Churches meeting, among his other obligations. And his contribution centred on disputing the assumption that economic growth should be the central organizing principle of society. "Growth was put in first place", Daly said, "because it would presumably wash away the problem of poverty in a cascade of abundance vouchsafed by the amazing grace of compound interest". But our chief fault has been the failure to recognize that any economy is only a subsystem of the "larger, finite, non-growing and closed ecosystem on which it is fully dependent".

When the expansion and growth of the economic subsystem threatens the carrying capacity of the whole, we are in trouble. Such growth, Daly and others contend, is actually "anti-economic", growth that impoverishes rather than enriches in real terms. Such anti-economic growth "makes it harder, not easier, to cure poverty, protect the biosphere... The Gross National Product continues to grow while welfare declines". And theologically, such affluent growth is a sin. Daly contends that "our ability and inclination to enrich the present at the expense of the future and of other species is as real and as sinful as our tendency to further enrich the wealthy at the expense of the poor... If it is a sin to kill and to steal, then surely it is a sin to destroy carrying capacity — the capacity of the earth to support life now and in the future".

From this point Daly proposes the alternative approach of "sustainable development", which means development in accord with the earth's environmental carrying capacity. Since the resources and raw materials of the earth are not infinite but limited, any economic systems must live within ecological realities or else threaten the foundations of life. Thus sustainable development ultimately redefines the meaning of development, delinking it from mere economic growth.

This provides only one way into the undergirding concept of "sustainable development". This phrase was on everyone's lips in Rio de Janeiro, prompting legitimate fears that it was just becoming another buzzword with no agreed-upon common meaning. Yet, the very discussion, with the readiness of so many to accept new language, indicates an honest search for new models and paradigms.

Initially, all the discussions about limits to growth beginning in the 1970s created suspicions among nations of the South that a new ideology was being set forth to allow the affluent to preserve their gains while denying such benefits to the rest of the world. While one could hear such fears persisting at points in the Earth Summit, more voices were acknowledging that the past model of development, with its undergirding assumptions, had failed. The need was not merely for new technologies and new funds transferred from the North to the South — but also for new goals, new models and new vision. That is what lies beneath the widespread attraction to the phrase "sustainable development".

The opening address at UNCED by Boutros Boutros-Ghali, Secretary General of the United Nations, reflected this quest for new vision. "The time of the finite world has come", he said, "in which we are under house arrest... Nature no longer exists in the classic sense of the term.... Every new triumph over nature will in fact be a triumph

over ourselves. Progress, then, is not necessarily compatible with life; we may no longer take the logic of the infinite
for granted. It is this great epistemological break which the
Earth Summit may ultimately symbolize for historians".

From there the Secretary General went on to offer his
own definition of sustainable development: "development
that meets the needs of the present as long as resources are
renewed or, in other words, that does not compromise the
development of future generations.... It forces us to
realize that, just as the countries of the South face problems in protecting the environment, the countries of the
North must likewise deal with the problems of over-
development".

Boutros Boutros-Ghali reinforced the theme that
economy and ecology must be understood as interdependent. In so doing, he referred to the Greek origins of both
words, from *oikos*, meaning the household. Eco-nomy
refers to the proper management of the household, while
eco-logy refers to the study and understanding of the
household. "They amount to the same thing: ecology is,
by its very nature, part of economy".

Those observations are hardly new to the ecumenical
movement. Theologians have often made the same point,
adding that the roots of the word "ecumenical" are the
same, referring to the one household of God. But the entry
of these concepts, familiar to many in ecumenical church
settings, into the heart of debate at a global event such as the
Earth Summit underscores the radical changes taking place
in how people at large grasp the contemporary global crisis.

Thus, the rhetoric at Rio signalled a growing global
consensus regarding the imperative of a changed understanding of what is meant by development, and of the path
towards a liveable future. Maurice Strong, the Secretary
General of UNCED, whose leadership over two years
shaped the course of this event, described this transition in
dramatic language: "The changes that come about as a
result of the shift to sustainable development will have an

effect as profound as anything that has taken place since the industrial revolution. Indeed, they add up to a veritable 'eco-industrial revolution' in which environmental considerations will more and more drive economic policy and industrial transformation".

So these days at Rio were filled with phrases of drama and vision. The concrete effect of all these words on policies and actions, of course, is a different question. Many worried that the Earth Summit amounted to little more than rhetoric. Yet the words were important, for they pointed to changes in global perception.

For those in the churches, the Earth Summit served first of all as a clear indication of how the world understands and articulates its present situation of crisis. And here, important lessons can be learned. For when the world's political leaders gathered as never before in history to address the questions of environment and development, what they heard and often what they themselves said was startling.

They acknowledged that the traditional path to development had failed. The assumptions that had been driving the programmes and hopes for global human welfare were called into sharp question. New approaches, values and models, all wrapped around the phrase of sustainable development, became a common commitment, even if its implications and meaning remained unclear.

This, then, is the first lesson to be drawn from the Earth Summit. Historians will regard it as a moment when the world began to speak of the failures of earlier dreams and to search for a new relationship between people, the earth and their economic activities. That search leads quickly into the terrain of values and ethics, and raises questions concerning spiritual realities. At issue is whether there is, in fact, a path which can lead the world to a future in which all people can be offered the hope of life and the earth can be preserved in its capacity to provide that life.

2. Ecology Is Global

Two decades before the Earth Summit, the United Nations called a Conference on the Human Environment, held in Stockholm, Sweden. That meeting came just as environmental issues were emerging in the awareness and on the political agendas of countries primarily in the North. The discussions there were an initial demonstration of the conflict between North and South over these questions.

Stockholm successfully placed environmental questions in a global perspective. Further, it enabled the United Nations bureaucracy to establish an international body for confronting global environmental problems, the United Nations Environment Programme (UNEP). Yet the lack of sufficient global consensus on environmental problems prevented strong and concerted actions.

The tensions at Stockholm were centred largely on the suspicion that environmental concerns are a luxury of affluent Northern societies. This fit the stereotype of environmentalism in those days. In the United States, for example, environmentalists were those who drove Volvos, ate quiche, wore earth shoes, and went hiking in wilderness areas on week-ends.

Talk of saving the earth at that time always raised the question of for whom the earth was being saved. And the assumption was that only those with money could afford to worry about dolphins and redwood trees; further, their concerns seemed self-indulgent.

At the level of political debate, nations of the South charged that environmentalism was another excuse for denying them the full opportunities and resources for industrial development that were central to many of their economic aspirations. Many resented what seemed like the imposition of a Northern agenda on their realities. And there was serious disagreement about the causes of environmental destruction.

Indira Gandhi of India addressed the Stockholm conference in 1972 with these words: "Poverty is the biggest polluter. If you are interested in us not polluting, help us get rid of our poverty". Many others echoed this view. And it asserted a basic confrontation between environmental protection and economic justice.

That tension dominated much of the international discussion in the years that immediately followed. It was also mirrored in ecumenical debates, making it difficult for the World Council of Churches to establish space in its theology and programmes for ecological concerns during those years. In various international discussions, the complaint was frequently made that industrial technologies and methods employed by the North were now being restricted to the South in the name of environmental protection.

Methods of ideological analysis also complicated these early debates. Those utilizing Marxist analytical tools — whether or not they were also supporters of specific Marxist governments — approached environmental problems first and foremost as a symptom of injustice between classes. For them, economics and power were the root causes.

This approach argued that environmental problems are simply a by-product of the global class struggle. In affluent capitalist societies, pollution resulted from control of the means of production by the wealthy classes and their vested interests. In the poor societies of the South, environmental damage was created because the masses of their poor had no power or control over economic resources.

Such a stance relegated environmental problems to secondary issues, or even pointless distractions. Efforts to address some specific ecological concerns were only "palliative measures", taking attention away from the "root causes". The real task was to understand and cooperate with those forces which were destined to defeat the power of the ruling economic classes. When societies were reconstructed on a classless model, giving the people ownership and control over production, environmental problems would fade away.

But as the world evolved during the two decades after Stockholm, a more global understanding of the ecological threat began to emerge. Discussions between the North and the South began to shift. The rigidity of ideological approaches began to be shaken. New perspectives began to emerge. Three reasons can be cited as influences.

First, a shift began occurring from specific environmental issues to global ecological connections. The environmental movement began chiefly around certain specific dangers and threats in particular regions, mostly in the North. Pesticides in the US were having unforeseen effects in poisoning foods and soils. Toxic wastes buried at Love Canal were having deadly effects on human health. Lake Erie, on the border between the US and Canada, was virtually "dead" from its pollutants. Acid rain from Europe's burning of coal was destroying forests and lakes in Scandinavia. And so on.

As long as environmental problems were seen as basically local, it was a matter of choice as to whether a given region or nation judged them to be of sufficient concern or not. And the division between attitudes of the North and the South seemed easier to justify. If Sweden wanted to worry about keeping wood wastes out of its rivers, fine for them. Meanwhile, Kenya had to worry about the price for its coffee beans on the international market.

But as awareness has grown of the inter-connectedness of environmental issues and of their links to the issues of development, the focus has turned to the limited "carrying capacity" of the earth as a whole. Ecology has been seen in its global dimension, perhaps best illustrated by the power of the image of the earth as a blue sphere floating in space: a single home, in which life is inter-connected. Damage, waste and greed in one place diminish life in other places.

Some specific issues make this connection with power and effect. The warming of the global atmosphere, while caused principally by the fossil fuels burned by affluent societies in the North, threatens a rise in sea levels and changes in weather patterns having global consequences, felt most severely in islands, coastlines and desert areas far removed from Düsseldorf or Cleveland. Likewise, preserving biological diversity, protecting forests, safe-guarding fresh water and controlling toxic wastes require international actions, not only local or national solutions.

Second, the two decades since Stockholm have seen the mushrooming of strong and effective non-governmental organizations in nations of the South, formed to study and mobilize action around environmental issues within their countries. Groups like the Centre for Science and Environment in India, headed by Anil Agarwal, were formed, conducting comprehensive studies on environmental issues, challenging development projects for their lack of ecological and cultural awareness, and engaging in widespread programmes of education and action. The Third World Network centred in Malaysia, with voices like Martin Khor Kok Peng and Vandana Shiva, emerged with publications, research programmes, news features and widespread efforts articulating perspectives from the South on development which is ecologically sustainable and meets the needs of people. The Green Forum in the Philippines, led by Maximo Kalaw, builds an extensive coalition of groups working for alternative, participatory and sustainable approaches to their future. Wangari Maathai coordinates the Green Belt Movement in Kenya, involving women in widespread grassroots efforts to replenish the forests and soils essential to livelihood.

Hundreds more like them have come into being. And their voices were at Rio, in the Earth Summit, articulating the urgency of the ecological crisis, integrated with the issues of social and economic justice, within their societies. Therefore, in the twenty years since Stockholm, the South has entered into the global debate on ecology, sustainability and justice, bringing the perspectives gained from the experiences within their societies. And political regimes in the countries of the South, increasingly pressured by movements of democratization, can no longer ignore the growing voices of grassroots groups mobilizing around these goals. As Wangari Maathai said to the government delegates in her address to the UNCED plenary session: "The nature of the environment and development debate has changed forever. UNCED has achieved the first step in the integration of these two concepts".

Third, the collapse of communist governments in the world opened new vistas in ideological debate and understanding of the global situation. The extent of ecological devastation under state socialism as practised in the former Soviet Union and Eastern Europe cast doubt on classical Marxist approaches to environmental issues. Indeed, attempts in those societies to establish general economic equity and to remove private ownership over the means of production provided no automatic protection against environmental ruin. If anything, there seemed in practice to be fewer effective restraints in those countries against measures which increased production at the cost of major ecological disasters.

Globally, it became far too simplistic to allege that environmental problems are only the symptom of economic disorder. The issues are more deeply inter-linked. Certainly, economic deprivation has resulted in environmental damage. But equally true, ecological deterioration has caused increases in poverty and human suffering.

José Lutzenburger, the fiery Brazilian environmental activist who also served for a time as Brazil's Minister for the Environment, said this to delegates at one of the official Preparatory Committee meetings for UNCED: "I heard one of the delegates repeating a common dogma of our development policies, namely that poverty is at the root of most of the environmental degradation we have today. But it is the other way around. Most of the poverty we see in the world today is the result of the destruction of traditional cultures, of the rape of their resources in the name of 'progress', of the uprooting of people who then are left with no choice but to vegetate in the festering slums or rape the last remaining wilderness".

His analysis strikes more deeply to the heart of the issue. The whole notion of progress, economic growth and industrialism, with escalating affluence, is the root of ecological destruction and the continuing economic impoverishment of millions. Both capitalism and Marxism, in their traditional forms, were built on these goals. For both, nature was nothing more than raw material in infinite supply, waiting to be transformed into something of value by the industrial process. Their argument rested upon who controlled the means, and thus enjoyed the fruits, of this production.

But today, the debate has become enlarged from ownership of the means of production to the means of production themselves.

At the Earth Summit, countries of the South, as well as most NGO groups from all parts of the world, focused attention on the ecological consequences of high levels of consumption, production, and unending growth of the industrialized countries. If anything, the changed ideological context in the world made the debate at Rio more open and creative.

Voices from the third world rightly continued to insist that the net flow of resources out of their societies to the North, through payments on foreign debt and terms of trade, had to be reversed if there was to be any hope of supporting initiatives of ecological sustainability in their societies. Few were willing to believe that an unchallenged and unrestrained global "free" market would magically usher in an era of sustainability. Many were pressing for a new global way of seeing together the issues of consumption, ecological preservation and economic equity.

Gamani Corea, Chairman of the Institute for Policy Studies in Colombo, Sri Lanka, served as head of the UN Preparatory Committee on Development Strategy for the 1990s. In preparations for UNCED, he warned against any consequence of sustainability which would imply two constant life-styles in the world — high consumption, industrialization and pollution in the North, and Gandhian simplicity in the South. "The real quest", Corea asserted, "has to be for a style of living which can be adopted by all countries, rich and poor, and consistent with the environment and the planet. It is for the rich countries to show the way for this life-style…. If the industrialized countries can show… a way of living and organizing economic activity and technologies which will be compatible with ecological harmony, it can be a universal model which all can emulate and strive to achieve". He argued for "replicable life-styles" as a more concrete expression and goal than sustainable development.

All this is fairly radical rhetoric for a United Nations meeting. Of course, when attempts were made to inject such ideas specifically into final documents, to be signed by one hundred heads of state, some affluent nations balked, positions began drifting apart, and diplomats searched for the lowest common denominators.

Tensions between the North and the South continued, though the terms of debate began to shift. Some nations of the South began insisting on recognizing how patterns of consumption and life-style were part of the problem rather than the solution. And while some countries, including several from the South, hotly defended their sovereign rights to do whatever they wished with their resources, others were clearly ready to begin acknowledging the truths of living, and sharing, in one common and increasingly fragile home.

Just the convening of the Earth Summit, and the enormous attention it generated around the world, was testimony to the recognition of the global reach of the ecological crisis. Specific trends emerging since Stockholm certainly contributed to this. Evidence of global warming and fears of its consequences became more persuasive. The six warmest years of the 20th century occurred during the 1980s. Nearly seven billion tons of carbon are dumped into the atmosphere each year primarily from burning fossil fuels, and the evidence suggests that the global temperature will rise because we have reached the limits of how much carbon can be absorbed by the earth's ecosystems. In other words, our use of fossil fuels, combined with deforestation, is no longer sustainable. And the effects are global.

The damage to the ozone layer is another example. Though 85 per cent of chlorofluorocarbons (CFCs) responsible for gradually rupturing this atmospheric shield are released in the industrialized North, the effects are global. Indeed, the first evidence occurred off Antarctica. The potential consequences are not only increased skin cancers, many of which would result in death, but also decreases in crop yields, fisheries, and other disturbances of ecological systems.

The loss of land further underscores the global nature of the ecological crisis. In a preparatory booklet for UNCED on "Environmentally Sustainable Economic Development" Robert Goodland points out that 35 per cent of all the earth's land is now degraded, and the trend is increasing, "a sign that we have exceeded the regenerative capacity of the earth's soil resource", even while hundreds of millions remain malnourished.

Examples could be multiplied. The point is that in the two decades between Stockholm and the Earth Summit in Rio de Janeiro, evidence became overwhelming that ecological damage is global in nature, binding North and South together either towards an escalating common tragedy, or on new paths towards a common, sustainable future.

After Gandhi had led India to independence, he was asked if India would attain the same standard of living as Britain. He replied: "It took Britain half the resources of the planet to achieve its prosperity; how many planets will a country like India require?" It has taken the world four decades of failed attempts at development, and evidence of destruction from pushing against the limits of the earth's inherent ecological capacities, to begin taking such statements with any seriousness.

3. The Spirit Is Willing, but the Flesh Is Weak

With two years of preparation and negotiations, and the focus of world attention, expectations around the Earth Summit were high. Further, its own agenda was as ambitious as any ever taken on by a United Nations meeting of this kind. So the pressure to announce the success or failure of UNCED was strong for journalists, delegates and NGO participants even before the event began.

From the point of view of the World Council of Churches, each of the three centres of activity around the Earth Summit provided a perspective for judging the significance of what happened during these days — the ecumenical gathering held in Baixada Fluminense, the Global Forum of thousands of groups and organizations, and the official government meeting, with its NGO observers, at the Riocentro. But the first question most people ask is, what was accomplished officially by the meeting of all these governments, culminated by the summit of heads of state?

The goals of UNCED were clear. First, a declaration, originally called an "Earth Charter", was to be adopted, allowing the international community commonly to agree on rights and obligations regarding the earth itself, with its present and future generations. Second, an ambitious and comprehensive plan outlining all aspects of sustainable development was drawn up in the preparatory process, and presented for final negotiation and approval at UNCED in Rio. Third, specific conventions, or international treaties, were envisioned dealing with particular global environmental issues such as climate change, biodiversity and forests. Fourth, decisions and commitments were expected from UNCED regarding the necessary funding of the new initiatives in sustainable development. Finally, UNCED featured discussion of what international institutions or mechanisms were necessary to implement these goals.

Within each of these areas, a complex system of international meetings, negotiating sessions, drafts and redrafts of various texts, and diplomatic bargaining set the stage, and had actually resulted in tentative agreements, with isolated points of remaining dispute, in almost all these areas by the time of UNCED. And in that preparatory process, non-governmental groups had an unprecedented degree of access and participation. The World Council of Churches took an active role in the process, sending delegations as an NGO to three official preparatory meetings, as well as to separate negotiating sessions on climate change, during the two years leading up to the final meeting in Rio de Janeiro.

Agreement on an Earth Charter as initially envisioned encountered several obstacles in the last months before Rio. Many, including Maurice Strong, the Secretary General of the Conference, and some delegations as well as many NGO groups, were looking for an inspiring document that could speak to the ethical, moral, and even spiritual dimensions of humanity's relationship with earth. But some governments began pressing more for a declaration on rights of development. Others were cautious about language that was too visionary. And by the last preparatory meeting, the process had reached an impasse.

The Chair of the Preparatory Committee, Ambassador Tommy Koh, pushed the diplomats during the last days of the preparatory meeting to formulate a set of principles from various proposals set forth in previous negotiations. This was made into the Rio Declaration, containing 27 principles. These include the "polluter pays" principle, the "precautionary principle" urging restraint from potentially environmentally damaging activities even when full scientific certainty is not present, and also the commitment to eradicate poverty and meet the needs of the least developed and most environmentally vulnerable nations. Also included, however, is a principle that states have "the sovereign right to exploit their own resources pursuant to their own environmental and developmental policies", as long as harm is not done "to the environment of other states or areas beyond the limits of national jurisdiction".

At the World Council of Churches meeting, a group of participants examined the final results of the Rio Declaration and called it "perhaps an appropriate compromise". Moreover, they stressed that some of its principles, if taken seriously and implemented, "provide the basis for significant and... even radical change". The document was adopted by governments simply as an agreed-upon declaration. As such, it has no formal legally binding character. But it can be used as a standard by churches and NGO groups in judging the actual practices of governments, and calling them to accountability on the basis of their own words.

The limitations of the Rio Declaration, however, were underscored by many, including Maurice Strong and Boutros Boutros-Ghali. They both urged follow-up steps to move from the Rio Declaration to the original goal of a full "Earth Charter" by 1995, to be signed on the 50th anniversary of the founding of the United Nations. The World Council of Churches and several other NGOs indicated their support of this process.

Agenda 21 is a 500-page document covering virtually every subject associated with sustainable development, suggesting strategies and steps by both governments, international agencies and United Nations organizations. Maurice Strong called it "the most extensive, comprehensive international programme ever developed and approved, word by word, by governments". Yet though adopted at Rio, it also does not have the status of legally binding actions. Instead, it represents the level of agreement reached by governments on actions they mutually believe are necessary for planetary survival and human welfare.

Most notable, however, is that such a comprehensive and far-reaching document was never originally planned by the UNCED Secretariat as one of the results. Rather, this came in the preparatory process as governments, as well as NGOs, brought an increasing array of issues to the table requiring action in some integrated approach. Thus, the final version of Agenda 21 signified the high level of expectations and inter-connected areas of needed global action which were brought into UNCED.

A review of its contents by chapter headings provides some indication of its scope. The document begins with an introductory appeal for *accelerating sustainable development through integrating environment and development in decision-making*. This includes establishing "systems of environmental accounting" and would integrate environmental costs and damages into measurements of economies. Then a section on *sustainable living* deals with combatting poverty, and "changing consumption patterns" as well as population, health and housing. Each of these areas contains pages of explanations, objectives and specific activities.

The next section of the document comprises 275 pages dealing with approaches to specific environmental issues: protection of the atmosphere, management of land resources, combatting deforestation, desertification and drought, sustainable mountain development, sustainable agriculture, biological diversity, and environmentally sound management of biotechnology. Some of these texts, such as that on the atmosphere, were debated in closed sessions late into the evenings at Rio, as nations like Saudi Arabia raised objections to the emphasis on "new and renewable sources of energy"!

Section III of Agenda 21 turns attention to the role of particular groups in achieving these goals. Individual chapters deal with women, youth, indigenous peoples, non-governmental organizations, workers and trade unions, business and industry, farmers, and the scientific community. And the final section deals with the "means of implementation", including structures for follow-up and the all-important question of finances.

Financial commitment for implementing Agenda 21 remained the most controversial issue throughout the process. The UNCED secretariat costed all the proposals, and estimated that the price of a transition to sustainable development would be about US$125 billion per year from now to the end of the century in the form of grants or concessional loans from richer countries to poorer ones. This would be more than double the present amounts of assistance for development flowing from donor countries.

The concrete step expected from the Earth Summit was far more modest — an initial commitment of between $6 to 10 billion in new funds directed towards these purposes. And by the end Maurice Strong reported that between $6 to $7 billion in new funds had been committed. Questions remain regarding the proposals for how these funds will be administered, and whether they will, in fact, unlock radically new approaches.

The Earth Summit produced two treaties, or conventions, which are legally binding on the nations which signed them. The first concerned reducing global warming, and the second dealt with the protection of biological diversity. And by the final day, 154 nations had signed each one.

The Framework Convention on Climate Change had been negotiated in sessions over the past two years. The main argument was over the specific deadline for reaching targets for reducing the levels of carbon dioxide — the chief "greenhouse gas" causing global warming — into the atmosphere. Proposals backed by the European Community, Japan and almost all of the developing countries called for establishing that, by the year 2000, release of carbon dioxide by developed countries would be no greater than the levels in 1990. The United States and some oil-producing countries opposed the setting of such specific targets. Compromise language was finally adopted setting the 1990 levels as a goal, without a specific target date. But the treaty also establishes a framework for continued negotiation and action on this issue.

The Convention on Biological Diversity aims at ensuring effective actions by nations to curb the destruction of species, habitats and ecosystems. Biotechnology firms would also be regulated, and a system established for dealing with access and ownership of genetic material, as well as compensation to developing countries for the extraction of their genetic materials. The Convention received widespread support but was opposed at the Earth Summit by the United States.

Author Vandana Shiva, a keen observer of the use of biotechnologies in developing countries, explained US opposition in this way: "The Bush Administration does not want the Earth Summit to put in place any international regulation on biotechnology. Rather, it wants to give industry a guarantee that they will have the licence to experiment and manipulate life forms, without any ethical, social or environmental responsibility".

The international press focused a great deal of attention on the role of the United States and President Bush at the Earth Summit. Certainly, one of the dominant features of the event was how badly the United States was isolated. But while it prevented a stronger climate treaty, and its refusal to sign the Biodiversity Treaty weakened its significance, the overall effect of US actions was to undermine respect for its role in global leadership, even from its most loyal allies.

Finally, UNCED adopted a statement of principles on forestry. While at earlier points the idea of a convention on this subject was also discussed, it became clear in the preparatory process that only a first step in that direction would be possible at Rio. However, a commitment was made to work towards a treaty dealing with desertification, an issue of urgency and importance especially for Africa.

Evaluating UNCED as an official governmental event, unique in history, can be done by asking three questions. First, did it focus the world's attention and commitment on the challenges of planetary survival? Here, UNCED definitely succeeded. Furthermore, new paradigms, approaches and ways of seeking an integrated understanding of justice and the integrity of creation were placed firmly on the global agenda.

Second, did UNCED succeed in mobilizing new commitments, agreements and actions by governments to reverse our present course, and concretely reshape the future? Only in part. That answer was even given by Maurice Strong, UNCED's Secretary General, in his closing remarks. A true Earth Charter is yet to be proposed and adopted. Agenda 21 is fine on paper, but must be implemented, including the issue of financing. The Climate Convention may lack sufficient strength at present to ensure reversal of global warming. The Biodiversity Convention lacks the agreement of the nation with the largest single power to erode its effectiveness. And other issues require international treaties as well to help reverse destructive trends. Yet, in all these areas, UNCED established a foundation for further action and ratified a new level of global agreement which had never previously existed.

Third, did UNCED provide a radical new departure that can ensure a sustainable future? Nothing guarantees this. Some NGO observers pointed to the inability of UNCED to integrate its actions with the crucial factors of international debt, the negotiations in the General Agreement on Tariffs and Trade (GATT), and the structures of foreign trade and exchange. While those questions came up frequently in discussions, little at UNCED mandates any breakthroughs in this area. Martin Khor Kok Peng of the Third World Network put it this way: "Many NGOs feel that by tackling sectoral problems such as water or toxic waste or habitat without addressing the structural causes such as the role of transnational corporations, the World Bank, the International Monetary Fund and GATT and without any serious discussions on the South's debt or poor trade terms, UNCED did not yield any results in terms of stopping the forces destroying both the environment and the lives of a large part of humanity".

David Hildyard, editor of the British journal *The Ecologist*, observed that "the North, which is primarily responsible for the crisis, is trying to get away with making as few changes as possible by blaming the South, whilst the South says it can't do anything without more money".

Certainly it would be naive to place all one's hopes for radical change in meetings and documents engineered by government diplomats through the UN system. The "spirit of Rio" was certainly very willing for creative change. But when government delegates sat in closed rooms to make commitments, it became clear that the "flesh was weak".

Recognizing the limitations of UNCED is just as important as noting its unique achievements. Whether or not UNCED serves as a step towards a new departure in history will finally be determined more by what happens in response to those fourteen days in Rio than by what occurred there.

At the closing session, Boutros Boutros-Ghali turned from the usual language of UN diplomacy to the world of spirituality in addressing the question of UNCED's significance. We have been told, he said, that we are to love our neighbours as ourselves, and this is true. But now we are learning that we must also love the earth. For thousands of years, the UN Secretary General told the diplomats and government ministers, ancient cultures believed that the earth had a soul, that we lived in a spiritual relationship with the world. And today we must restore that sense, in order to build a new ethical and political context to live and act with the earth.

At a press conference immediately after the close of UNCED, Maurice Strong came back to a central point. "We cannot sustain current life-styles in affluent countries.... The present economy is simply not sustainable. The evidence is powerful, and must get through to the people. The status quo will not survive".

Strong ended by stressing that UNCED gives a basis for making fundamental changes, but alone it is not enough. "Political will is the problem, and mobilizing such political will is the key". In that process, the role of NGOs and groups will be the source of hope and action.

The experience of the thousands of groups, organizations, movements and NGOs at Rio de Janeiro during the Earth Summit was highly creative and upbuilding. They debated the issues, drafted their own versions of treaties and conventions on critical issues, built new alliances, identified the weaknesses of the official process, and made far-reaching commitments to ongoing political action around the world.

History may well judge that the forces set in motion at the Earth Summit were far more decisive in mobilizing the people, groups and movements who were not a part of governmental structures. Their actions may prove, in the long run, to be more important in building a sustainable future than the documents and treaties signed at Riocentro.

4. The Letter from Baixada Fluminense

"It is as though Christ the Redeemer is calling to those officials at Riocentro with his right hand, and telling them to turn their attention to where he is pointing with his left hand, to Baixada Fluminense", Archbishop Dom Mauro Morelli said in welcoming the participants in the World Council of Churches meeting. He had invited the delegates from WCC member churches around the world to hold the meeting in Baixada Fluminense in order to encounter the real life of the people of Brazil and the vital witness and ministry of the local churches. Many had feared that the thousands coming to the Earth Summit would never meet Brazil as it really is.

But this decision was not without difficulties. It meant that for the first half of the Earth Summit, the WCC's participation would be geographically separated from the centre of the Global Forum, as well as from the official government meeting at Riocentro. Coverage by journalists would be extremely difficult, as well as access by visitors curious to know the perspectives of the WCC on the Earth Summit. Yet it meant that this ecumenical meeting would find its context in the life of churches in Brazil and their ministry to the social, economic and spiritual needs of the people. And that seemed to be the proper setting from which to view and to interact with the Earth Summit.

A two-year history of WCC involvement in the UNCED process lay behind the gathering at Baixada Fluminense. It had been encouraged at the outset to help organize the participation of international religious groups as one sector of the non-governmental organizations in UNCED.

The WCC called together a wide coalition, which established itself as the Working Group of Religious Communities on UNCED. It included not only other Christian organizations concerned with the issues of UNCED, but interfaith bodies and representatives of groups from the world's other major religious faiths. Partners included the World Wide Fund for Nature (WWF), the International Coordinating Committee on Religion and the Earth, the World Conference on Religion and Peace, World Vision International, and about twenty other groups in addition to the WCC. This coalition reviewed the UNCED agenda, and identified first of all deliberations on the proposed Earth Charter as a place where religious communities might have a unique contribution to make.

Immediately prior to the Third Preparatory Committee meeting for UNCED, which took place at the United Nations in Geneva, Switzerland, this Working Group called together a gathering of fifty people representing various religious traditions and organizations from around the world. Meeting at the WCC's Ecumenical Institute in Bossey, outside Geneva, they focused their attention on the Earth Charter and presented a proposal, "One Earth Community", to the official government delegations who were beginning serious deliberations on this topic. The World Council of Churches played a major role in facilitating this event.

By that time, however, it was clear that the foremost responsibility of the World Council of Churches was to educate, assist and strengthen its own member churches in their awareness of UNCED and their local response to the global issues which it was addressing. As the WCC observed the UNCED process and listened to its local churches, four issues emerged which claimed priority: (1) continued attention to the Earth Charter; (2) strengthened church participation among voices from the South within the non-governmental preparations for UNCED; (3) increased emphasis on the inter-connections between environmental preservation and economic justice, as highlighted in the WCC's Justice, Peace and the Integrity of Creation (JPIC) process and the Canberra Assembly; (4) attempts to influence ongoing governmental negotiations on a climate change treaty, an area of priority action identified by the WCC's JPIC world convocation in 1990.

To this end, the World Council produced a series of resources for the churches, including a booklet, "What is Your Church Doing about UNCED?", and a video, "Together in the Garden", which highlighted these emphases and attempted to help churches reflect on Christian witness in light of the crisis of environment and development. WCC delegations were sent to the women's preparatory meeting for UNCED — the "World Women's Congress for a Healthy Planet" — as well as to each of the government negotiating meetings on the climate change treaty and to the official Preparatory Committee meetings for UNCED.

This background of work, however, made it clear that the Earth Summit itself in Rio de Janeiro called for a major presence of the ecumenical community from churches around the world. This was not based on the hope of influencing the outcome of decisions reached by governments while at Rio. The WCC had recognized that its primary opportunity for having any such impact was during the four official Preparatory Committee meetings, where NGOs had a high level of respected participation. By Rio, however, most decisions were made, and those still in doubt were largely in the hands of government negotiators meeting in closed sessions.

Rather, the Earth Summit called for a representative gathering of the churches of the world in order to bring their perspectives, offer their response, and establish their commitment to the questions brought before UNCED. The voice of the global Christian community needed to be heard in that setting. But more than that, churches around the world had to be informed and strengthened in their own response, as communities of Christian faith, to the global crisis of environment and development. Moreover, the churches needed to be amongst the thousands of organizations and groups gathering in Rio to build common commitments for the sake of the earth's future.

For the World Council of Churches specifically, and the ecumenical movement in general, there were additional reasons for convening during the Earth Summit. The WCC had made a major commitment to "the conciliar process of Justice, Peace and the Integrity of Creation". This called upon the churches to make major commitments, or covenants, with one another in response to the threats facing humanity and the earth. The Canberra Assembly of the World Council of Churches in early 1991 reaffirmed this commitment. Yet what this actually meant for the future programmes and work of the WCC remained unclear.

The Earth Summit thus represented an opportunity for the WCC to express further its commitment to Justice, Peace and the Integrity of Creation, as well as to clarify what this might entail in the future in light of the world's present situation. It was also a unique occasion for the ecumenical movement to judge and test its own actions and the shape of Christian witness in the face of the world's own understanding and assessment of contemporary challenges.

Throughout the seven days in Baixada Fluminense, worship together, structured around the "bad news" of ecological destruction, poverty, militarism and the "good news" of God's promise and action in Jesus Christ, was one of the richest experiences shared by the participants.

From the start, the ecumenical group was also deeply connected with the worship and life of the local churches. On the first evening, hundreds welcomed the WCC participants in a worship service at the Nova Iguaçu cathedral, during which youth, black people, the elderly, women and others shared accounts of the daily oppression which marks their lives. And yet, all was in the context of hope and unaccountable joy, nourished by fellowship and worship in a Christian community of boundless grace, courage and love.

"Searching for the New Heavens and the New Earth" was the title of the WCC meeting. For many, the first sign of where to begin this search was in the life of those Christian communities who were experiencing faith, hope and encouragement in the face of crushing problems. The issues confronting the Earth Summit finally require not just technical and political answers, but the strength and power of the Spirit of God evidenced in the Christian communities and churches like those in Baixada Fluminense, who had opened their lives to the pressing needs of their society and offered God's empowering love to the victims of the world's injustice.

The programme of the WCC meeting was designed to take the perspectives and commitments emerging from the JPIC world convocation in Seoul, Korea, and apply them to the UNCED agenda. Seoul had produced inter-linking "covenants" dealing with four areas: global economic justice, militarism and peacemaking, preserving creation, and combatting racial oppression. Thus, the WCC agenda at Baixada Fluminense featured presentations dealing with each of these issues in the context of the Earth Summit. A theological reflection team sought each day to focus on the biblical and theological dimensions of the discussion. From that basis, the participants were to decide on the nature of their response to the Earth Summit.

The result was most illuminating and instructive. First, the participants decided that their most important task was to write a letter to the churches from around the world, offering to them their discernment, encouragement and challenge coming out of this encounter with the Earth Summit. World Council of Churches meetings are famous for producing official, and at times uninspiring, reports and documents. But here the participants wanted something different. They wanted to reach out with a word that would speak to and strengthen churches in their efforts to respond to the groans and cries of creation. This letter, like the worship of the meeting itself, centred on the coming of the Spirit at Pentecost, for the Protestant and Catholic celebration of Pentecost came on June 7, halfway through the Earth Summit.

The Letter to the Churches declared: "Dear sisters and brothers, we write with a sense of urgency. The earth is in peril. Our only home is in plain jeopardy.... We dare not deny our own role as churches in the crisis which now overwhelms us. We have not spoken the prophetic word ourselves. Indeed we did not even hear it when it was spoken by others". It goes on later to affirm, "Our God is a God of life, and the power of the Holy Spirit permeates all creation. Therefore, we should develop a spirituality of creation.... To live according to the Spirit is to capture its presence in all creation.... Our churches themselves must be places where we learn anew what it means that God's covenant extends to all creatures..." (see Appendix 1 for the text of the Letter to the Churches).

The Letter was written with the style and tradition of the early church's epistles in mind. The tone and intention was for representatives of churches, meeting at an historic occasion, to write to churches scattered throughout the globe, offering interpretation and counsel to assist in their discipleship and witness. The authors hoped that the Letter could be used in the worship and liturgy of local congregations as well as in conferences and publications.

Halfway through the meeting at Baixada Fluminense, the participants identified the areas which had emerged from presentations and discussion for their further consideration and recommendations. These included the UNCED Conventions, population and environment, militarism, the role of the churches, economics, pollution, theological questions, and education and communication. Each participant was then asked to choose those areas where he or she most wanted to work in a small group. The result was striking. The first three areas chosen by far were the role of the churches, education and communication, and theology.

Thus those who gathered at the WCC meeting felt that the most urgent tasks for an "ecumenical response to the Earth Summit" were to strengthen the role of the churches in addressing these questions, to further the ways of educating and communicating these issues within the Christian community, and to give attention to the theological questions involved. The specific substantive issues of economics, militarism and global warming were certainly of deep concern as well. But this meeting seemed to be marking an important transition in ecumenical gatherings.

For those at Baixada Fluminense, attention became focused on specific ways to strengthen the witness and action of the churches themselves in the face of the crisis revealed by the Earth Summit. This seemed more urgent and important than passing resolutions or reports that analyzed the issues. Perhaps this was because there was general agreement around the nature of the problems which the world faces. Or perhaps it was because participants sensed that, in the long run, inspiring and challenging churches to concrete commitments was a far more important response to the Earth Summit than issuing more documents detailing the problems which face the world.

At the same time, the meeting's presentations and its final recommendations did give considered attention to very specific concerns. All this was in the context of attempting to express a guiding vision and ethic: as explained in the Letter, "we have worked together this week on the vision of just, peaceful, and ecologically sustainable development in a life-centred world society".

That work encompassed a focused examination of the links between racism and the effects of environmental destruction. It also gave special attention to the role of indigenous peoples in the search for sustainable societies. Questions receiving relatively little attention at the government meeting, such as the effects of militarism on the earth today, were brought into sharper focus at Baixada Fluminense. And some issues overlooked in previous WCC meetings, such as the relationship of population, consumption and the environment, received attention at this ecumenical event. Finally, participants at Baixada Fluminense, including several who had followed UNCED developments closely over the past two years, offered an overall evaluation of UNCED's successes and shortcomings at the official level, and suggested what this might mean for the churches' future work (see Appendix 2 for the text of this report).

On the final evening, the participants were drawn once more into the worship life of the local church communities. It was the eve of Pentecost, and the WCC representatives were invited to join with hundreds in the cathedral of Duque de Caxias for an all-night vigil. Songs, celebrations, prayers, testimonies, sharing from the WCC participants, a meditation by theologian Leonardo Boff, as well as breaks for food and fellowship, continued through the night.

Then, from a liturgical bonfire in the courtyard of the Cathedral, all lit torches and candles and processed through town, joined along the way by hundreds from other parishes, until five or six thousand were gathered for a sunrise Pentecost service in the town square. Praise was offered, petitions for the earth and the Earth Summit were shared, scripture was read, Emilio Castro preached, and Eszter Karsay, a Reformed Church pastor from Hungary, blessed bread which was distributed to all. The Letter to the Churches, approved by the WCC meeting after final revisions the previous afternoon, was read on that Pentecost morning, and copies were given to representatives of each of the regions of the world, symbolizing the sending forth of that word to all corners of the earth.

No official UNCED meeting took place at Riocentro that Pentecost Sunday. The thousands of government delegates had the day off. Many were comfortably sleeping in well-appointed hotel rooms along Rio's beaches, far from the town square Duque de Caxias in Baixada Fluminense. But between those two places, Christ the Redeemer watched; and many prayed for the wind of God's Spirit to blow that Pentecost morning through many dry and drowsy bones in Rio de Janeiro.

5. Seoul, Canberra and Rio de Janeiro

When Emilio Castro, General Secretary of the World Council of Churches, addressed the ecumenical meeting at Baixada Fluminense, he asked: "What impact will this gathering have on the 400 million Christians in the churches of the WCC around the world?" Moreover, he pressed the question of how the Earth Summit will affect the ongoing work of the ecumenical movement. As the UNCED is evaluated, as NGO groups plan their actions in the wake of the Earth Summit, and as the message of the WCC meeting at Baixada Fluminense is shared, several central challenges for the ecumenical movement become clear.

These challenges did not originate at Rio. They draw on many streams of past ecumenical thinking and commitments. In particular, the results of the Seoul world convocation on Justice, Peace and the Integrity of Creation in 1990, and the work of the Seventh Assembly of the World Council of Churches held in Canberra, Australia, in 1991 set forth directions that help to interpret these issues. Nevertheless, the Earth Summit brings fresh urgency, creativity, and new perspectives as it underscores several challenges now clearly facing the ecumenical movement.

Spirituality

Rarely, if ever, has the concern for spirituality been so evident, both officially and unofficially, within the atmosphere of a secular, international gathering such as the Earth Summit. Hannah Strong, wife of the UNCED Secretary General Maurice Strong, chaired a "sacred heart conference" bringing together spiritual insights from indigenous peoples and various religious traditions on the eve of the official meeting. A declaration from that gathering presented to the UNCED delegates read: "The planet earth is in peril as never before. With arrogance and presumption, humankind has disobeyed the laws of the Creator which are manifest in the divine order".

That initiative continued during the official UNCED conference as a presence of "Wisdom Keepers" was maintained at a retreat centre near Riocentro. There, with fire and drum beats, people were invited to gather for meditation and prayer throughout the time of UNCED. And the organizer of an NGO briefing at Riocentro one day invited surprised listeners to give her their requests for prayer and meditation to take back to the group at the retreat centre.

The Global Forum in downtown Rio drew a wide spectrum of religious groups. Most notable was an all-night vigil, ending with an inter-religious service at dawn, addressed among others by the Dalai Lama. Nearly sixty groups representing different religious traditions gathered in tents in Flamengo Park to pray, meditate and practise their own forms of worship through the evening. The variety of spiritual practices was so diverse and, depending on one's perspective, bizarre that it stretched the limits of religious tolerance. Evangelical Christian groups from Brazil, for instance, wanted to participate in the vigil, but chose to remain separated on the other side of a fence as they expressed genuine doubts over suspected witchcraft and other "spirits" being worshipped in some of the practices.

Some Pentecostal and evangelical churches in Brazil expressed little faith or interest in all the events surrounding the Earth Summit. But a rally calling such Christians to show their praise for God as the Creator drew tens of thousands into the streets of downtown Rio one afternoon.

A panel discussion at Riocentro on the day before the heads of state summit began included Mahbub Ul Haq, a noted international economist from Pakistan, now serving prominently with the United Nations Development Programme. He said NGO participation at UNCED stressed, among other things, that the spiritual dimension of environment and development must be recognized, rather than just material factors. Part of the challenge, he stated, was "making these values more respectable".

What, then, does this mean for the world's churches, and their work together in the ecumenical movement? The challenge is twofold.

First, we must nurture and offer our spiritual response to the crisis of environment and development. When Emilio Castro was asked what the churches bring to the Earth Summit discussion, he answered: "First of all, Jesus Christ". He meant this not in an exclusivist, narrow way which would separate faith from social and political action. Rather, the churches bring the faith of belonging to the body of Christ, following the One through whom the whole world has been claimed by God's redeeming love. Thus the churches bring to these issues, above all, their spiritual conviction, their faith and their hope in God's promises and power.

It is easy to be apologetic about spirituality. Many, perhaps, find it more comfortable to write documents, reports and analytical papers which set forth the correct political positions of the churches and the ecumenical movement on pressing issues. All that is necessary, and of value. But those at the Earth Summit expected and even asked the religious communities to give something more — to share the power of their spirituality and to nurture this as a foundation for overcoming the deep causes which destroy the earth and consign millions to desperate poverty.

The resources touched upon in worship and liturgy during the WCC meeting at Baixada Fluminense, as at Canberra and other ecumenical gatherings, give a clue to the power of this dimension. The persistent requests from Canberra and the World Council of Churches' Central Committee to deepen biblical, theological and ethical reflection on work dealing with justice, peace and creation also point to the desire to establish more spiritually enduring roots for the churches' acts of engagement with the world.

A perennial problem of the church is that spiritual concerns are often associated exclusively with personal piety and sacramental acts, separated from prophetic social witness and political action. One clear lesson from the Earth Summit is that such a separation will prevent the churches from bringing the contributions which they can most uniquely offer to the hope of building a sustainable future.

But a second part of this challenge also confronts the churches — that of discernment and clarity in the midst of so many widely divergent expressions of spirituality. What is the response of the churches to the contemporary quest for spiritual resources of vision and values to address the joint crisis of environment and development? Not every "spiritual" answer offered to this crisis is helpful. Some may indeed worsen the situation by suggesting misleading escapes from realities. So while the church welcomes the world's search for spiritual sensitivities and resources, it does not do so uncritically.

A central calling of the churches today is to develop a spirituality of creation. That requires reaching deeply into neglected streams of Christian traditions, as well as discovering the promptings of the Spirit in the wonder and the pain of the earth. That discovery can be enhanced by listening to the witness of other spiritual traditions as well.

The task, then, becomes one of testing, discerning and shaping spirituality for Christians today which enables us to participate in our hearts with God's redeeming love for the earth and all its people. The issue of gospel and culture, which has aroused fresh interest in ecumenical discussions today, finds a concrete test in dealing with spirituality and creation. Moreover, critical theological questions also arise — questions which sharpen the urgency of ecumenical attention to the theology of creation. As we shall see in the next chapter, the necessity of this theological quest by the churches was powerfully reinforced by discussions at Baixada Fluminense, at the Global Forum, and at Riocentro.

Refocusing the JPIC process

As originally envisioned at the WCC's Vancouver Assembly, the conciliar process on justice, peace and the integrity of creation had three general purposes: (1) to approach these issues understanding their inter-relatedness to one another; (2) to encourage mutual commitments (covenants) by the churches to these urgent issues of survival, based on the imperatives of Christian faith; and (3) to discover new avenues towards Christian unity through this process of mutual commitment. While interest in JPIC has grown in the churches since the world convocation at Seoul in 1990, the next concrete steps for the WCC in advancing the JPIC process have been unclear and indecisive. The Earth Summit underlines the need for the WCC to refocus the JPIC process with concrete programmes and efforts in the years ahead.

Rio demonstrated that fathoming the inter-connections between ecology and economy is imperative if ways to a sustainable future are to be found. And UNCED underscored the necessity of redefining our concepts and approaches to development. On these points, the ecumenical movement needs to listen to where the world is in its discussions and understandings.

Debates attempting to separate economic justice from environmental concerns and to prioritize them in distinct programmes are still heard within the ecumenical movement. Creative exploration of alternative models and values for societies has not yet burst forth from the initiatives of the World Council of Churches. And while Canberra called in February 1991 for development of "an ethic of economy and ecology", almost prophetically predicting discussions at the Earth Summit, the WCC had done no work in this area by the time of Rio.

In other areas, the JPIC vision can offer insights and connections neglected by discussions at Rio. Three specific examples can be mentioned:

1. *Militarism and sustainable development:* One valid criticism of the Earth Summit was the relative lack of attention given to the impact of militarism on the global crisis today. The problem of financing the costs of sustainable development aptly illustrates the issue. The estimated costs, as noted previously, for a global transition to sustainable development are $125 billion a year from now to the year 2000. If industrialized nations all agreed to meet the suggested target of giving seven-tenths of one per cent of their Gross National Product as assistance to developing countries, $150 billion a year would be available. But only fractions can be found at present — $6 to $7 billion of new funding. Yet global spending for military purposes is at least $1 trillion per year.

The JPIC process has asserted, from the beginning, that justice and a restored creation cannot be severed from peacemaking. That truth must be pressed by the ecumenical community into national and international discussions of how the world can move towards a sustainable future.

2. *The contribution of indigenous peoples:* From the time of the Canberra Assembly, the history of suffering of indigenous peoples — often in the name of Christian mission — and their rights and place within societies today, have entered deeply into the concerns of the ecumenical movement. At Baixada Fluminense, these perspectives were a powerful part of the gathering. Indigenous peoples took part as well within the Global Forum, and increased global attention is beginning to be given to their situations and perspectives. The World Council of Churches can build on its commitments from Canberra to ensure that the voice of indigenous peoples is heard within the search for sustainable societies.

3. *Racial justice and environmental preservation:* One of the four covenants at the Seoul convocation dealt with

the churches' commitment to racial justice. Yet racism has often remained as an isolated, although crucial issue within ecumenical concerns. At the meeting in Baixada Fluminense, examples were shared of the practice of disposing of toxic wastes in areas with high populations of racially oppressed people. Such patterns can be found within North America as well as between countries. This signals one way in which the churches can relate the urgent quest for racial justice to the healing of the earth.

Finally, the churches' participation in the Earth Summit provided a clear example of how JPIC can lead to new paths and experiences of Christian unity. The best illustration, perhaps, comes from the interaction between the World Council of Churches' involvement in UNCED and the Roman Catholic Church, which is not a member of the WCC.

At the outset of the WCC's involvement in the UNCED process with other religious organizations, a formal invitation was sent to the Vatican inviting them to participate officially in this process. They declined, stating that because they are officially represented in the United Nations as a state (rather than as a non-governmental organization), they would participate in UNCED only through this means.

The decision was a disappointment to the World Council of Churches, since it ruled out official collaboration on questions such as the Earth Charter, on which the views of the Vatican were in fact quite similar to those of other churches and religious groups.

However, when the National Council of Christian Churches in Brazil agreed to act as the local hosting body for the WCC meeting during the Earth Summit, this opened a different door to cooperation with the Roman Catholic Church, at the local level. The result was rich interaction with the Roman Catholic Church in Baixada Fluminense. During the course of those seven days, the common community of the Spirit created between

Orthodox, Protestant and Catholic, and encompassing cultures from throughout the world, was profound.

At the Pentecost sunrise service, thousands gathered to worship, pray and share bread. Technically, it was not an official eucharist. (Archbishop Dom Mauro Morelli had said, "let the theologians decide those questions".) But it was an experience of unity so deep that Emilio Castro declared in his sermon that Baixada Fluminense would, from now on, be known as "the ecumenical capital of Brazil".

What brought about this experience of unity were not discussions of doctrines to reconcile theological or historical differences. Rather, it was the common commitment to act together, at the Earth Summit, in response to the threats to justice, peace and the integrity of creation, because of a shared faith in the gospel of Jesus Christ. And as the participants explored, shared, prayed and worshipped together, expressing faith commitments in the face of the global crisis which had called the world to Rio, a new level of Christian unity was discovered which made other doctrinal or structural barriers seem irrelevant and obsolete.

The experience was a metaphor for JPIC as a conciliar process. It demonstrated how work together on these issues can create vitally new experiences and expressions of Christian unity. All of this seems to transcend what could be accomplished, in the case of UNCED, through diplomatic negotiations between Geneva and the Vatican.

The ethics of sustainability

The rhetoric and the inspiration of the Earth Summit reached for a new model to redirect the course of development and to ensure ecological sustainability for the future. The question has become one of how to accomplish such goals. And this involves a fresh exploration of what ethics and values are to guide this process, and how they can actually affect economic, social and political practices.

If economic systems are to be geared towards sustainability, rather than depletion, of the earth's carrying capacity, how is this to be accomplished? What is the role of
markets in allocating resources? And what of state inter-
vention? What political mechanisms are needed to con-
strain resource depletion? How are equity and justice to be
established without relying on unlimited economic
growth? How can short-term costs be adjusted to reflect
the true long-term values of air, water, soil and biodiversity? Guiding ethical principles are necessary to help
answer such questions.

The World Council of Churches, and especially its
JPIC process, has provided incisive prophetic critique of
the threats facing global survival. Churches have been
empowered in their ability to denounce the reigning
powers of injustice and destruction. But the next step has
been more difficult: what counsel and guidance can be
offered to societies searching for new alternatives? What
advice and wisdom do the churches have to offer regarding ethical values that would clarify political programmes
and economic choices faced by societies?

The Earth Summit highlighted the global urgency of
this discussion, and challenged the ecumenical movement
to give new attention to the hard work of defining ethical
perspectives and values that shape political and economic
decisions necessary for a sustainable future.

An interfaith context

Participation within a global process like the Earth
Summit underscores the pluralistic religious environment
which characterizes the world and shapes the context in
which the churches seek to contribute and work. Previous
WCC programmes of dialogue with people of other living
faiths have focused on building relationships of understanding and learning, exploring openly points of tension
and difference, and reflecting on the implications for the
understanding of mission. But as churches involve them-

selves ecumenically in the global issues presented by the Earth Summit, they find themselves side by side with those from other religious traditions who come with similar concerns for the planet's future.

Lessons can be learned from the history of the WCC's involvement with the UNCED process. It began with an attempt to build an interfaith coalition, as described previously. This bore important fruit through creating a network of various religious groups concerned about UNCED. It was easy for Christian groups and participants in that process to play a dominant role. Establishing an interfaith approach which more truly reflects the world religious pluralism is difficult because of basic differences in style, organization, representation and commitment among the various religious groups.

Second, interfaith efforts associated with the Earth Summit, and issues of ecological preservation, have a tendency to move rapidly to the lowest common spiritual denominators in language and approach. This is possible in part because one can discover considerable convergence among the world's major faiths concerning sacred responsibilities and values involving the creation. As such, this constitutes an important arena for interfaith cooperation.

Yet the temptation of such efforts can be to quickly seek an eclectic and inclusive form of religious consensus which bypasses the work of each religious faith in relating its own tradition and beliefs to the global crisis of environment and development. Thus, certain interfaith approaches to the challenges of the Earth Summit seemed broadly inspiring and unifying to some, but felt alien to others because there seemed little place for any particular contribution of their own religious faith.

In addition, the experience of the World Council of Churches was that its member churches were clearly looking for assistance on how to relate their Christian faith and witness to the questions of the Earth Summit. Thus, educational efforts were devoted to this end. And the decision was made to meet for the first seven days at the Earth Summit specifically as a Christian community, to deepen its own understanding and response to the issues at hand.

Only after taking this first step was the group ready to explore, and seek its role within, interfaith initiatives at the Earth Summit. Several WCC participants did so in encounters during the following days at the Global Forum. This included one focused seminar examining interfaith initiatives to date and formulating a common message to UNCED.

Thus, the Earth Summit challenged the ecumenical community to take its concern for interfaith dialogue into the realm of concrete cooperation and action around its global agenda. But at the same time, it learned that such an approach is not fruitful unless the churches are first called to deepen their understanding and engagement with these issues as intrinsic to their Christian witness. This commitment is essential in providing the basis for the contribution which the ecumenical community can then make to interfaith cooperation.

Churches, NGOs and movements

One of the WCC's tasks is to nurture the relationships between its churches, including those movements and groups providing challenges, resources and inspiration for the renewal and deeper faithfulness in the churches' mission and witness. Today specifically, this means identifying those new groups and life-giving examples that have a genuine capacity for renewal in the ministry of the churches and their outreach in the world. What was at the "frontier" of the church and of society twenty years ago no longer plays that same role today. All this became particularly clear at the Global Forum in Rio de Janeiro.

Two decades ago the World Council of Churches launched significant initiatives to express concrete support for efforts at social and economic justice throughout the world. At that time, the role of non-governmental organizations in working for social change was still relatively weak, although growing. The WCC made a major commitment directly to support the efforts of such groups and "movements" working for fundamental change in their societies.

Such commitments sometimes created tensions between the role of the WCC member churches and the Council's support for a growing number of groups and movements that were working largely outside the church and separate, in some cases, from any declared sense of Christian identity. At times, stereotypes were created which reinforced a direct conflict between institutionalized member churches and such grassroots movements. And many committed to the WCC's leadership role in prophetic work for justice championed relationships to such movements as the primary means for implementing this calling.

The massive participation of NGO groups, organizations and movements at the Earth Summit demonstrated how much has changed in the last twenty years. An explosion of NGO groups in all corners of the world has occurred, mobilizing energy and commitment of millions of people working for changes in their societies and the world. And some of the most creative and impressive growth has come in new NGOs working on the challenges of environment and development.

Thus, the ecumenical movement no longer needs to play a leading role in stimulating and supporting the development of such groups. That is already happening on a wide scale. The question posed at the Earth Summit was how the churches, and the WCC, find their new role and contribution in light of this changed situation. Discerning the WCC's distinctive place in this new context is essential.

It will serve little purpose for the WCC merely to duplicate creative work for justice and sustainability already being done by numerous other groups. Further, it would be a strategic mistake today to assume that the WCC's contribution to the global quest for survival will come through mobilizing movements and groups rather than engaging its own churches in this struggle.

The wide variety and involvement of organizations at the Global Forum illustrated clearly that the churches have new opportunities for building creative, challenging and mutually supportive relationships with various groups as a means to strengthen the churches' contemporary mission and prophetic witness in the world. This requires abandoning the old stereotypes that forced choices between movements or churches. It further calls for the WCC to evaluate realistically the established "networks" of relationship to groups that have become institutionalized over the past two decades. Its task now is to discover both fresh partners and new patterns of mutual relationships between the WCC's member churches and "movements" that are fresh potential sources of renewal in the churches' life and witness.

The rich diversity and growth of organizations present at the Global Forum provides grounds for hope. But it also challenges the churches to enter into the global arena with their distinctive vision, faith and contribution, offering what they can give uniquely in the midst of this diversity.

Life-style and consumption

The Earth Summit drew major attention to questions about life-styles — and patterns of consumption which are the result — in the world's affluent societies. This became a critical and contentious issue. Representatives of developed countries worked hard to resist and dilute references to such issues within Agenda 21; and the earlier negotiations over an Earth Charter broke down in part over this issue. Yet the final result is that the Earth Summit's discussions raised probing questions and critiques of the patterns of consumption which reign in developed societies.

Both global justice and ecological sustainability require fundamental changes in production, consumption and life-style among those who disproportionately control and enjoy the world's wealth. Yet such changes strike at the core of human behaviour. The role of religious faith in this process is indispensable. In the end, the control of greed, and the attraction of living a life that is in harmony with creation's gifts and resources, requires spiritual commitment and inspiration.

In this respect, the Earth Summit presents a fundamental challenge to the ecumenical movement. Can the churches see the issue of life-style and consumption as a basic question of faithful global discipleship and spiritual practice in our day? Can the ecumenical movement provide the world with models and examples that will fill others with hope and inspire their responses as well?

In the past, questions of life-style have generally been relegated only to churches in developed countries, and for obvious reasons. Further, any focus on changing life-styles has often been suspect for not addressing changes in global economic structures. But discussions at the Earth Summit revealed that the questions of consumption are, indeed, issues of global survival. It was voices from the South which pushed this agenda in the official debate. And many in the NGO groups called for new and sustainable models of consumption and life-style which could be emulated in both North and South.

The fresh analysis coming from the Earth Summit is that the questions of production, unlimited economic growth, reckless consumption and destructive life-styles are fundamental to changing global economic structures. The obligation of the churches is to consider how this challenge can become a part of their spiritual life and practice.

6. Redeeming the Earth

Brazilian theologian Leonardo Boff is one of the leading figures in the development of liberation theology. His many books, especially *Jesus and the Poor*, have been important in shaping a theological movement which places the economic oppression of the poor and their struggle for liberation at the foundation of interpreting the meaning of the Bible and the social practice of Christian faith.

As a Roman Catholic priest in the Franciscan order, Boff's views were not always pleasing to the authorities in Rome. On several occasions, he was asked by the Vatican not to do any writing for a period of time. Early in 1992, while he was on a sabbatical leave, Franciscan authorities said they would prefer that he not return to the Brazilian university where he has taught for nearly twenty years. Just after the Earth Summit, Boff announced that he had resigned from the priesthood and from the Franciscan Order. He took this step, he said, "not to be free from the church, which I love and shall never abandon, but to be free to work without impediment.... One cannot breathe without air, one cannot create without freedom".

Before this announcement, Boff had been invited to address the WCC gathering in Baixada Fluminense on the theology of creation. Recently, he had been devoting study and attention to this subject, anticipating issues that would be raised by the Earth Summit.

Boff's interest in the theology of creation was especially significant because in the past liberation theology had paid scant attention to the themes of creation and ecology. In some ways, its emphasis on the historical acts of God in the liberation of people from bondage was in conflict with theology stressing God's work of creation, and the gift and grace of God manifested in the intrinsic goodness of all things in the created order.

But the powerful presentation Boff gave at Baixada Fluminense demonstrated the rich theological integration taking place today, which is overcoming the previous divisions between liberation and creation. He outlined an approach which brought together Orthodox insights regarding the sacramental sanctification of the material world, traditional Catholic perspectives, views of process theologians, insights from feminist theology, a vision of the cosmic scope of Christology, and the contributions of liberation theology to provide a deep and integrated understanding of God's creation and the response of the church to its present crisis.

Leonardo Boff's contribution illustrated how developing a theology of creation is ecumenically rich and promising. Many of the divisions within the ecumenical community around other questions seem bridged when the focus becomes the understanding of creation. Several World Council of Churches meetings, including the Canberra Assembly, have emphasized the importance of furthering reflection on the theology of creation as a major ecumenical study project.

The Earth Summit illustrated both the potential richness and the urgent need for such theological attention within the ecumenical movement. The theological reflections and common affirmations, as well as the points of controversy, shared at Baixada Fluminense can serve as a guide to future ecumenical work to be undertaken. Key issues which emerged can be briefly summarized, but require careful work in the months and years ahead.

The place of humanity in creation

A general ecumenical consensus has emerged in recent theological attention to the ecological crisis which affirms humanity's responsibility to care for and to live in harmony with God's gift of creation. Older views attempting to give biblical sanction to humanity's unbridled right to "subdue" the earth in any way necessary have been largely rejected in favour of fuller theological perspectives underscoring biblical affirmations of the intrinsic goodness of creation.

Yet this movement has not resolved the more pressing question of the place of humanity within the whole of creation. Humans are distinct and unique. But does that imply a hierarchy which places humans above all other parts of the creation, and then constructs a system of values accordingly? Are humans to be emphasized as the centre of creation, from which to judge the significance of the rest of life? And from that, does the primary human response towards the creation consist of managing, controlling and acting as a responsible steward?

Or, in the interpretation of biblical passages like the last chapters of Job, or certain Psalms, are humans given a far more humble place within the creation? Is the primary reality the interdependence of all life, rather than the independence of human life? Does not the unfolding of the creation itself, with a scope beyond human imagination, and a rich history of millions of years of life preceding humanity, present a revelation that centres on God's glory, and mocks human pretensions to control and define the centre of value for the life of the universe?

Since the Seoul world convocation, calls have come in ecumenical gatherings for developing, in the words of Metropolitan Kirill of the Russian Orthodox Church, a "new Christian anthropology", to clarify the meaning of being created "in the image of God". And the questions and tensions concerning the human relationship to the rest of creation were clearly evident at the Earth Summit — within the official declarations of governments, among NGOs, and at the ecumenical meeting in Baixada Fluminense.

The Rio Declaration adopted by UNCED begins with this first principle: "Human beings are at the centre of concerns for sustainable development". And yet, many ecologists and theologians have argued that it is precisely such an "anthropocentric" view, isolating humanity from the whole of creation and seeing humans as the source for measuring all value and progress, which has brought us to the ecological peril now threatening all life — and especially human life.

The report of the Theology Group from the ecumenical meeting at Baixada Fluminense argued this way: "We affirm the goodness of God's creation and the intrinsic worth of all beings. Anthropocentric, hierarchical and patriarchal understandings of creation lead to the alienation of human beings from each other, from nature, and from God. The current ecological crisis calls us to move towards an eco-centred theology of creation which emphasizes God's spirit in creation (Genesis 1:2, Psalm 104), and human beings as an integral part of nature" (see Appendix 3 for full text).

Orthodox theologians have stressed that it is through Christ that the whole created world is brought into the scope of God's redeeming love, and that humanity thereby is to play the distinct role of offering and referring the creation back to God in thankfulness, respect and reverence. Thus, discussions at the Earth Summit emphasized the need for exploring more fully the theological perspectives on humanity's place within the creation.

The material and the spiritual

The Letter to the Churches from Baixada Fluminense declares that "the Spirit inhabits the whole cosmos, gives breath to all life, and tunes our hearts to hear the heartbeat of the earth and the way of truth and beauty. What is opposed to the Spirit, then, is not the material and the world, but rather sin and the power of death".

The emphasis on a fuller understanding of the Holy Spirit, which was central to the Canberra Assembly with its theme, "Come, Holy Spirit — Renew the Whole Creation", has brought forth rich theological and biblical reflection concerning the relationship of God's Spirit to the creation. While other forceful theological perspectives in the 20th century had emphasized God's transcendence and "otherness", the focus on the Spirit leads to the intimate connections, reflected in many biblical passages, of God's Spirit with the creation.

Leonardo Boff, in his presentation to the WCC meeting, quoted this saying: "The Spirit sleeps in the stone, dreams in the flower, and becomes awake in humanity". And so, Boff stressed, "the Spirit inhabits the cosmos. Thus, we announce nature as creation, a cosmic dance of the elements, a new re-enchantment of creation".

But for many, questions still remain. How holy is the creation? How is an awareness of the Spirit's presence within the material world distinguished from worshipping the earth as sacred? Has the power of sin and death infected the nature of creation itself? Or has it only distorted humans in their relationship to creation?

During debate on the text of the Letter to the Churches, one Orthodox delegate referred to the phrase: "We should include the material elements in our celebrations and praise the cosmic symphony the Spirit continually composes". He worried that this sounded too much like syncretism, recalling debates from the Canberra Assembly. Yet, as another Orthodox delegate had pointed out in an earlier presentation, each year the Orthodox celebrate a liturgy of blessing the waters, and this holy water is then taken from the service to homes and fields as a sign of the blessing of creation.

It is one of the ecumenical ironies today that Orthodox voices are often among the first to warn of potentially syncretistic theology and practices. Yet on the other hand, they are the foremost in bringing elements of the material and cultural world into the heart of their liturgies through a profound understanding of the Spirit's indwelling presence in all creation.

When Boff, the Catholic liberation theologian, was challenged on his description of how the life of the Spirit permeates all creation, he replied by quoting resources and teachings from Orthodox theology. This was but a sign of the cross-fertilization which characterizes the search for theological explorations of creation. Yet the relationship of the Spirit to the material world, which is central to developing a Christian spirituality of sustainability, raises theological anxieties which require fresh biblical reflection and careful attention.

Hierarchy vs ecology

Feminist theologians in particular have stressed the deep connections between hierarchical understandings of authority and the destruction of the environment. The same interpretation of scripture which allows some to say that men are the masters over women justifies the rape of the earth as a necessary duty. Such systems of authority and value arrange the world around God as above and apart from the earth as King, men as vice-regents, women and children as their servants, indigenous people as savages to be civilized, animals as valuable only to be hunted and killed, and nature as the wild world to be conquered and subdued.

Such a view also reinforces a dualistic understanding separating the mind from the body, the spiritual from the material, and male from female. All this enshrines a mindset and system of values rooted in masculine authority, coercion and domination. Women, nature and people of colour all are the victims.

From this perspective, an ecological approach stresses relational and holistic understandings that move beyond hierarchy, overcome dualism, and establish equality and community. Such views have been expressed widely among those reflecting theologically on feminist perspectives and ecological problems.

The deeper theological issues involved, however, come back to the relationship of God to the world. An ecological or relational model, as opposed to a hierarchical model, rests upon an understanding of a deeply interdependent relationship between God, humanity and the whole of creation. God is present within the relationships of all creation, and with humanity, rather than being outside and apart.

But even while affirming these perspectives, questions remain regarding God's transcendence, God's judgment, and God's action in bringing about a new future. Does the strong affirmation of God's presence within and amongst the creation obscure the power of God's judgment on present evil and hope in future promises?

Kwok Pui-lan, a theologian from Hong Kong, coordinated the theological reflection team at the Baixada Fluminense meeting. She has written powerfully concerning the connections between feminist theology and ecological solidarity. In addressing the question of God's action in bringing about "the new heavens and the new earth" — the theme of the conference — she replied that in Western Christianity, questions about eschatology always deal with "when". But today, the focus should be on "where" and "how".

Moving from hierarchical to relational and ecological understandings of the creation, for the churches, finally must be rooted deeply in our views of the Trinity. Here again Leonardo Boff's contribution during those days was most helpful. He spoke of the understanding that all life — human and non-human — is bound together in a covenant, a community. And this, he said, "relates to the intimate nature of God — the communion of the three divine persons of the Trinity in one God; the universe lives from this communion, and is celebrated in this sacramental life of the Trinity".

Ongoing theological work dealing with the issues of hierarchy and ecology, then, must become rooted in the relational life of the Trinity, upholding the life of the world. A challenging and crucial ecumenical task today is to bring into dialogue certain streams of classical Trinitarian theology with the new perspectives of feminist and ecological theology.

Creation and liberation

Perhaps the most encouraging theological developments from the Earth Summit were the signs that a new integration was emerging between the classic concerns for liberation and the crucial importance of theology of creation. Leonardo Boff's contribution was prominent in this regard. But several other voices also pointed in the same direction.

Among these were the perspectives of indigenous peoples. Their outlook begins with the primacy of their relationship to the creation. Thus, their understanding of liberation is inseparable from restoring creation and living in a manner which sustains it.

Native American theologian George Tinker has argued that the kingdom or reign of God, as spoken of by Jesus, rests in a renewed relationship with the creation. The space or place to find this kingdom in our midst is more important than asking when it will come. He questions past approaches to liberation theology whose focus on the historical process has prevented attention to present relationships with creation.

Thus, new voices, including many heard at the Earth Summit, are endeavouring to build theological approaches which overcome the division between creation and liberation. This mirrors, of course, the wider efforts at UNCED and the Global Forum to transcend the old debate between environment and development.

Developing a theology of creation which reflects this integration has the potential to be rich and empowering for the ecumenical movement. First, this can undergird and integrate the approach to justice, peace and the integrity of creation. Beyond this, such a theology provides a basis for understanding and cooperating with persons of other faiths. And a theology of creation developed in this manner can provide a new basis for deepening the search for unity among the churches.

At the close of Boff's contribution at the ecumenical meeting, he spoke of the "new alliance of humanity and creation.... For the new heavens and the new earth, new men and women must be created. We must bring about new people in a new covenant with creation, venerated and restored. For this creation is the temple of God". Work to deepen the theology of creation ultimately has as its task the nurture of such new people living in covenant with creation.

7. Sustainable Society

The search for a sustainable society is nothing new for the ecumenical movement. In the mid-1970s, the World Council of Churches launched a major programme titled the "Just, Participatory and Sustainable Society". This was an effort to provide a vision and sense of undergirding guidelines for churches in their efforts to work for social and political change. As the title suggests, the attempt was to integrate the urgent demands for global justice with the participation of people in building a future which would be sustainable.

Early discussions of the "limits to growth" contributed to the vision of sustainability within this programme. But the effort was not without its difficulties. During those years, as was noted previously, aspirations for development and global economic justice were often polarized from discussions of sustainability. And other theological problems concerning the role and identity of the church within the movements for radical political change eventually brought this WCC programme to a premature halt in 1979.

Yet, the World Council of Churches was successful in stimulating a global discussion around justice and sustainability which continued in many arenas. In fact, the concept and term "sustainability" was given its initial definition and meaning within these ecumenical discussions. The World Council of Churches played what later proved to be a prophetic role in focusing attention on the questions of sustainability, and its relationship to justice and participation, during those early years.

The historical irony is that after ecumenical tensions officially curtailed the JPSS programme, these ideas took on a life of their own, eventually becoming widely discussed in secular global circles. Even though "sustainable society" was no longer part of any ecumenical slogan or programme, it had become by the late 1980s the watchword of new thinking about patterns of global development. In 1987, the UN World Commission on Environment and Development, chaired by the Prime Minister of

Norway Gro Harlem Brundtland, issued its landmark report, *Our Common Future*. This document focused global attention on the concept of sustainable development, arguing the imperative of such an approach in both the North and the South, as well as outlining costs and obligations imposed upon the rich in order for this transition to be a reality for the poor. From that point on, the challenge of sustainability became a governing concept in global discussions, even while debates about its meaning, and the changes which it truly required, gathered strength.

The World Council of Churches launched its conciliar process on Justice, Peace and the Integrity of Creation (JPIC) in 1983 in part to set forth a new approach to fill the void left by the demise of the JPSS programme. But as that effort unfolded, particularly as the Canberra Assembly in 1991 developed these concerns through its four subthemes, including "Giver of Life — Sustain Your Creation!", a new emphasis was placed on the vision and values for sustainable societies. Recommendations came for working on an ethic of ecology and economics, for exploring "sustainable value systems", and for grasping both theologically and in practice the intrinsic connections between economic justice and ecological preservation.

Thus, at the Earth Summit, ecumenical thinking and global awareness seemed to come together in a new point of convergence. But the course in the future becomes critical to chart. Certainly, the first task for the ecumenical community will be to deepen the commitment, theological understanding and concrete engagement of churches in work for sustainable societies. Beyond this, the ecumenical movement has opportunities to challenge and shape the ongoing global search for a sustainable future. Important examples can be highlighted.

An Earth Charter

As we have seen, this became an initial focus of ecumenical attention to UNCED, carried out through important interfaith initiatives. But the Earth Summit left the task far from complete.

The parallel frequently drawn to illustrate the potential importance and influence of an Earth Charter is the Universal Declaration of Human Rights, composed and ratified in the early days of the United Nations. The views of religious groups had an impact on its formulation. In fact, one of the groups involved in drafting the declaration was the Commission of the Churches on International Affairs (CCIA), later part of the WCC.

Over the years, the Universal Declaration of Human Rights has emerged as an important international standard, both to judge the actions of governments and to advocate the cause of those unjustly treated. While it does not function as a specific international legal instrument, its effect has been substantial. This is further strengthened through the United Nations Commission on Human Rights, which functions to monitor situations throughout the world, and subjects governments to certain levels of accountability and pressure. Non-governmental groups, including the World Council of Churches, play an active and recognized role in the Commission.

The hope of many is that an Earth Charter would play a similar role in declaring internationally "rights" of the earth for its preservation and respect, and the obligations of all nations towards future, as well as present, generations. Such a Charter would attempt to draw, therefore, on resources of moral and ethical reflection common to humanity. Further, the theological and spiritual foundations from the world's religious traditions would play an important role in helping to set forth the vision and orientation of such an endeavour.

During the preparatory stage of UNCED, efforts towards this end began to grow. Initially, government delegations did not take the proposal with much seriousness compared to other items emerging on the UNCED agenda. Yet Maurice Strong, as Secretary General of

UNCED, consistently emphasized this as one of the chief goals of the Conference. He stressed that an Earth Charter needed to set the broad framework of moral commitment, from which the other action plans and treaties would follow.

Several non-governmental groups became strong advocates of an Earth Charter in meetings of the preparatory committee, however, and were responsible in part for focusing the attention of various government delegations on this question. By the third preparatory committee in August 1991, there were at least a dozen initiatives being undertaken by various NGOs in drafting potential Earth Charters, and holding consultations in various parts of the world.

The World Council of Churches made a contribution to this process through the draft proposal "One Earth Community" (see Appendix 4), which came from an interfaith meeting that gathered together various suggestions and initiatives. Members of the UNCED secretariat addressed the meeting in Bossey, Switzerland, which drafted this proposal. Copies were shared with government delegations, and a WCC spokesperson was given time, as an accredited NGO representative, to address the official preparatory committee.

As government delegations turned their attention to the Earth Charter, some wanted a visionary document. One suggestion was even for a poet to be found to draft an Earth Charter that would "sing" and inspire. Other delegations wanted specific legal principles simply to be listed. And then, the overall conflicts in the UNCED process between the North and the South began to be played out in suggestions for an Earth Charter.

Little progress was made. By the time the third preparatory committee meeting ended, the chairman had produced a "consolidated draft" containing the interventions from various governments, which was 18 pages long with 136 paragraphs.

At the final preparatory meeting, negotiations ground to a halt, especially over northern resistance to language addressing consumption and life-style issues, and the insistence of some developing countries on language ensuring their sovereign rights over their resources. Clearly, the process was falling far short of the original vision of an Earth Charter establishing a basis of moral inspiration and commitment of rights or obligations for the earth and future generations.

The Rio Declaration, drafted at the last minute as a compromise solution, was the result (see Appendix 5). While it includes many important principles that can ensure international consensus around responsibilities for environment and development, it is a far different kind of document in content, style and function from what was originally envisioned.

The commitment to something far better was clearly made by UNCED. As summarized earlier, Maurice Strong and the UN Secretary General have urged a continuing process to draft and agree upon an Earth Charter by the 50th anniversary of the United Nations in 1995. Here, the ecumenical community, particularly through the World Council of Churches, has an important opportunity for taking a leadership role among NGOs. It can help to gather the spiritual inspiration, moral vision and global political support for an Earth Charter which could serve as a powerful international standard by which nations can be committed and held accountable to building a global sustainable society.

The Sustainable Development Commission

The task of implementing, monitoring and coordinating the agreements of governments reached at Rio will be given to a new Sustainable Development Commission which UNCED has recommended be established. While follow-up work to build on the Earth Summit will be shared by many official and unofficial international bodies, within the United Nations system this Commission will have a primary responsibility. Its proposed structure will follow in some ways the United Nations Commission on Human Rights, and will feature active participation by non-governmental groups.

Thus, the World Council of Churches will have an important institutional link available for acting on the particular concerns, points of advocacy, critiques and challenges which it brings to ongoing international efforts to further sustainable development. All the particular issues and treaties brought forth from Rio, including the Earth Charter, implementation of Agenda 21, further steps under the Climate Change and Biodiversity Conventions, and efforts towards treaties on forestry and desertification, will be coordinated here.

But in the post-Rio world, the ecumenical movement should press the discussion of the criteria for and ethics underlying sustainable development. Widespread global support for this concept does not necessarily mean agreement over its precise definition or its concrete effects on economic and ecological practices. Therefore, the discussion of the values and ethical principles on which to build sustainable development becomes an important avenue by which the ecumenical community engages in its follow-up to the Earth Summit.

Some examples from the discussions at Rio can be cited. Herman Daly proposed at Baixada Fluminense that four terms could constitute an ethical foundation: sustainability, sufficiency, equity and efficiency. He explained, "Growth has become unsustainable. It has never been equitable in that some live far above sufficiency, while others live far below. No system that uses resources at a rate that destroys natural life-support systems, yet without meeting the basic needs of all, can possibly be called efficient". He suggests searching for economic policies which would allow these values to be put into practice.

Leonardo Boff questions even the use of the term "development". He fears that "sustainable development" is being used as a term "organized around the paradigm of continued and unlimited development, but essentially in its economic dimension... there is always conflict, which is resolved in terms of development and not of the ecology". Boff proposes instead to speak of the goal as sustainable *society*. He further explains, "We need a more profound, holistic ecology which sees the human being as part of a whole and which aims to respect this whole, which understands that to aggress against Nature is to aggress against oneself".

On the other hand, development economists like Jan Pronk, Minister of Development Cooperation for the Netherlands, who has had close ties with the ecumenical movement, argues that sustainable development means a different quality or kind of growth. "The current emphasis on quantitative growth should certainly be replaced by more concern with qualitative growth. But this should not be confused with zero growth, which is largely a sterile and disruptive dialogue".

This simply indicates some of the parameters involved in exploring ecumenically the ethics of sustainable development. But in these months and years after Rio, the ecumenical movement is compelled to be involved in this exploration. Certainly the concept which the World Council of Churches helped to originate almost two decades ago should now receive ecumenical energy when it is defined and applied by the world.

In the post-Rio work on sustainable development, the ecumenical community also must consistently lift up those connections which must remain central. Chief among these is the devastating external debt soaking up the financial resources, draining the internal capacities and distorting the economies of many nations of the South. As long as there is a net transfer of over $50 billion a year from poor to rich nations, the capacity for achieving sustainable development will not be present.

The same may be said of the world's ongoing addiction to military expenditures in the post-Cold War era. Ecumenical work for sustainable development must continually emphasize the links with debt, terms of trade and military spending, demonstrating the interdependence of justice, peace and the integrity of creation.

Finally, following the analogy of global action on human rights, watchdog groups and organizations have a crucial role to play. The work of Amnesty International, for instance, has had a major influence on human rights policies and influenced decisions of the UN Human Rights Commission. A similar network of groups must be put into place to reinforce the efforts of the UN's proposed Sustainable Development Commission. And the World Council of Churches is uniquely equipped to draw on its global membership from over one hundred countries to monitor, from local situations, whether national and international commitments to a sustainable future are being implemented, and are having effect.

Climate change and other UNCED conventions

The Seoul JPIC world convocation made four specific covenants. The one dealing with integrity of creation pledged action by churches on the threat of global warming and climate change. In response, churches and ecumenical groups worked to monitor the international negotiations on a climate change treaty leading up to UNCED, to influence the positions of governments particularly in the affluent countries, and to encourage changes in life-style and energy use.

That process has proved to be fruitful and effective. A major meeting of churches, mostly from Europe and North America, held at GATT in early 1991 sparked widespread interest. Monitoring teams sent by the World Council of Churches to the negotiating sessions distributed position papers, interacted with delegates, and their views were covered in the press. This helped to create some sense of moral urgency around the issue of global warming.

It would be a mistake to over-estimate any concrete effect of these efforts on decisions reached by governments. Yet the churches, through the WCC, have established themselves as knowledgeable observers and participants in this process. Their informed positions, interest and commitment are being noticed. And within some nations government officials take this with seriousness.

As the global warming crisis continues, and nations move under the obligations of UNCED's Convention on Climate Change to take steps reducing releases of "greenhouse gases", while negotiating future measures, the involvement of the churches in this process, facilitated by the WCC, will take on increased importance. In particular, the ecumenical movement can bring into this process the voices from churches and groups in those areas which will be the first victims of global warming, such as low-lying islands in the Pacific and elsewhere.

A similar pattern of ecumenical involvement is possible around the biodiversity treaty signed at Rio, and the process towards treaties dealing with forestry and desertification. Furthermore, as the UN prepares for the World Population Conference in 1994, the World Council of Churches should prepare its contribution, as recommended by the gathering at Baixada Fluminense.

The commitment to work for a treaty on desertification is the one main achievement for Africa to emerge from UNCED. As steps are taken towards international agreements addressing the causes of the devastating expansion of desert regions, especially in Africa, the ecumenical movement can support its churches and partners in that region in pressing for action to follow up swiftly on Rio's good intentions.

In all these areas — global warming, biodiversity, forests and desertification — the ecumenical movement need not pretend to offer technical expertise. Rather, it can offer its moral and ethical expertise, clarifying the choices available to policy-makers, and calling them to values and standards which treat the earth as the common and precious gift of God for all. Only that goal, continuously held before those entrusted with international decisions, will enable sustainable societies to emerge as a global reality.

* * *

So Christ the Redeemer stood with arms outstretched, looking with pathos and compassion at Baixada Fluminense, the Global Forum and Riocentro during those fourteen days of the Earth Summit. Were he to speak, what would he say?

Certainly, he would denounce those practices and powers which allow 1.2 billion people to remain poor, while the ratio of the wealth of the top 20 per cent to that of the bottom 20 per cent of the world's population has grown to 150 to 1. Certainly he would denounce how this same model of "progress" turns forests into deserts, depletes and destroys soil, disrupts the atmosphere, poisons water, and puts into peril the God-given foundations of life. And he would say that these are two inseparable sides of one sin — turning away from God as the giver of all life

But he would also announce good news. He would say again that he came offering abundant life. He would declare God's promises and covenant with all creation. He would ask us to remember the lilies, challenge us not to store up wealth in our barns or banks, and declare that those in bondage are to be set free.

Finally, he would offer to us his redeeming love. A love that draws together Riocentro and Baixada Fluminense. A love that suffers with homeless black children on Rio's streets who fear for their lives. A love that embraces earth, air, fire and water, yearning to bring forth a new creation. A love which calls together a community formed by the Spirit, which lives by the power of the resurrection and testifies to God's faithful embrace of all life in a world that is our common home.

Appendix 1
Letter to the Churches

Baixada Fluminense, Brazil, Pentecost 1992

To our brothers and sisters in all the churches, grace, mercy and peace to you in the name of the Crucified and Risen Christ! We have constantly given thanks for you and remembered you as we gathered in Brazil this Pentecost season 1992. A candle has burned continuously in our midst, bearing the light and life and hope we share with you. It burned from the opening moments of praise to our God in worship each day, throughout our deliberations, and until we joined the fire of thousands in the night vigil and the dawn procession celebrating their Pentecost. With you we have prayed for the Holy Spirit to fall gently upon the peoples gathered for the Earth Summit, to inspire our sons and daughters to prophesy and to fill the young with visions of justice and the old with dreams of healing this wounded world. This very same Spirit leads us to recognize, in creation, the One who "makes springs gush forth in the valleys", who "brings forth food from the earth", who "stretched out the heavens like a tent" and "set the earth on its foundations" (Psalm 104). This Spirit acts in all the cosmic elements, fills the universe with the glory and energy of God, and animates our own hearts with enthusiasm for all that is creative, good, right and noble. For this Spirit of life, we praise God!

Remembering you, we have gathered as Protestants, Roman Catholics, Orthodox and Anglicans — Christians from fifty-four nations at the World Council of Churches' conference, "Searching for the New Heavens and the New Earth". For years many of you have been engaged in the conciliar process on Justice, Peace and the Integrity of Creation. Committed to this vision, we have laboured to respond in faith and hope to the momentous issues of the Earth Summit, the United Nations Conference on Environment and Development.

Dear sisters and brothers, we write with a sense of urgency. The earth is in peril. Our only home is in plain jeopardy. We are at the precipice of self-destruction. For the very first time in the history of creation, certain life support systems of the planet are being destroyed by human actions.

Here we have seen this again at Baixada Fluminense, State of Rio de Janeiro. Visiting communities we have seen signs of hope of the poor who struggle against poverty and oppression. For this area is known for deep degradation of life conditions for the majority of the population. Poverty and violence are overwhelming against human beings, along with high levels of environment-degrading pollution. This was symbolic for us, for wherever human beings are denied their God-created dignity, the rest of creation is denied its dignity also. It is as though the terrible vision of Isaiah were taking place in our midst. "The earth lies polluted under its inhabitants; for they have transgressed laws, violated the statutes, broken the everlasting covenant... Therefore a curse devours the earth, and its inhabitants suffer for their guilt" (Isaiah 24:5-6a).

Brothers and sisters, you understand why our hearts are heavy. UNCED is meeting twenty years after the Stockholm Conference on the Environment and not one single major trend of environmental degradation has been reversed. All life today is endangered to a far higher degree than twenty years ago. We are fearful about even more brutal facts twenty years from now. For we continue to assault the planet. Consumption of energy continues as though it were limitless in content and benign in effect. Many animal and plant species have been brought to extinction. Pollution of water, soil and air is greater than ever. Desertification and deforestation accelerate. Vast sums for weapons and militarization continue to drain desperately needed resources and the practice of the powerful to use local conflict for political and economic purposes, after the ending of East-West confrontation, has escalated. The burden of the debt of poor countries has become more and more stifling. Hunger afflicts more and more people, not only in Asia, Africa and Latin America, but also in the Eastern European countries, the Middle East, the Far East, the Caribbean, and even within the affluent nations of the so-called "first world". Economic policies imposed upon already impoverished countries strangle the possibility of survival for multitudes of people. And the children, what shall we say to the children and to generations to come?

We have come inevitably to the conclusion that the prevailing system is exploiting nature and peoples on a worldwide scale and promises to continue at an intensified rate. You will understand why our hearts are heavy and why it is extremely urgent that we as churches make strong and permanent spiritual, moral and material commitments to the emergence of new models of society, based in deepest gratitude to God for the gift of life and in respect for the whole of God's creation.

Towards this end we have worked together this week on the vision of just, peaceful and ecologically sustainable development in a life-centred world society and send, with this letter, our detailed recommendations to the churches on many of the issues that now imperil us and all life. As well, we implore members of churches to urge their national governments to sign the UNCED declarations and conventions, and to implement their decisions.

We dare not deny our own role as churches in the crisis which now overwhelms us. We have not spoken the prophetic word ourselves. Indeed, we did not even hear it when it was spoken by others of late, including a number of scientists. Much less did we hear the cries of indigenous peoples, who have told us for centuries that modernity would foul its own nest and even devour its own children. So we need to mourn and repent. We have offended our God, "maker of heaven and earth", and we have blasphemed life and one another. We have come to our senses only very late, and do not do so even yet. We have brought the harsh judgment of even the infinitely Compassionate and Merciful One upon us, for our massive neglect, injustice and destruction. We plead for forgiveness and pray for a profound change of heart, a radical turning from the way of death to God and the way of life.

For there is hope (2 Corinthians 4:7-12). Our God is a God of life, and the power of the Holy Spirit permeates all creation. Therefore, we should develop a spirituality of creation. Biblically, spirituality means to live according to the Holy Spirit. The Spirit is the giver and sustainer of life. All that fosters life, such as justice, solidarity and love, and all that defends life, such as the evangelical commitment to stand with the poor, the struggle against racism and casteism, and the pledge to reduce armaments and violence, concretely signifies living according to the Spirit. This is more than a political act for the Christian, it is spiritual practice. Even more, to live according to the Spirit is to capture its presence in all creation. For, as we said early on, the Spirit inhabits the whole cosmos, gives breath to all life, and tunes our hearts to hear the heartbeat of the earth and the way of truth and beauty. What is opposed to the Spirit, then, is not the material and the world, but rather sin and the power of death. And where we must always begin is with veneration and respect for all creatures, especially for human beings, beginning with those most in need. The Spirit teaches us to go first to those places where community and creation are most obviously languishing, those melancholy places where the cry of the people and the cry of the earth are intermingled together. Here we meet Jesus, who goes before, in solidarity and healing. Here we receive, and give, bread for the hungry, water for the thirsty, joy for the needy, consolation for the grieved. It is here we offer our true spiritual worship as members one of another (Romans 12:1).

Our churches themselves must be places where we learn anew what it means that God's covenant extends to all creatures, by rediscovering the eco-centric dimension of the Bible. This means a modest material life-style that loves and treats the earth gently, as God does. At the same time, we should include the material elements in our celebrations and praise the cosmic symphony the Spirit continually composes. As we do so, we should cultivate a penitential attitude for the sins committed against nature and nurture compassion for the beings we harm (Philippians 2:1-5). We should fashion relationships of inclusion and reconciliation between the sexes, between races, cultures and peoples, maintaining a posture of blessed anointing before each being and the whole body of beings. For remember, dear sisters and brothers, we are the body of Christ and members of the cosmic temple of God. Let us pray during this Pentecost season, then, for the Holy Spirit to come upon us afresh. Let us cry out with all our being, "Come, Holy Spirit, Renew the Whole Creation!"

From delegates and observers
of the World Council of Churches meeting,
"Searching for the New Heavens and the New Earth:
An Ecumenical Response to UNCED"

An Evaluation of the
UNCED Conventions

Prepared at the WCC meeting, "Searching for the New Heavens and the New Earth: An Ecumenical Response to UNCED", June 1992

Within their understanding of justice, peace and the integrity of creation, churches approached the Earth Summit convinced of the need for action to protect the well-being of all creation and to redress the inequities which perpetuate poverty in so much of the world. In UNCED, we recognize both achievement and limitations. For the first time, the world community was gathered to deal with the inter-related crises of ecological destruction and global poverty. However, the results of UNCED are an inadequate response to the seriousness of the crisis.

Churches have been involved in issues of environment and development for many years and will continue long after UNCED. They view UNCED as one point in a long process to bring about ecological sustainability and economic justice. The scope of UNCED's Agenda 21 is an illustration of the long-term nature of the issues. Given the urgency to make progress, churches have an important role in witnessing with their people about the changes needed to achieve just, equitable and ecologically-sustainable development. Ecumenical networks among churches including the JPIC network will be crucial in facilitating church follow-up of UNCED.

a) The Rio Declaration

The WCC and some member churches were active in the early negotiation stages of UNCED in providing input to what was proposed as an "Earth Charter". The Rio Declaration, which was the outcome of those negotiations, is perhaps an appropriate compromise among the positions advocated by various countries. The Declaration acknowledges human responsibility to care for the planet as a whole; it recognizes that the ecological crisis is caused largely by the industrial and consumer practices in developed nations; and it calls for greater international cooperation to address problems of environment and development.

Many of the principles (e.g. preventive principle, "polluter pays" principle) provide the basis for significant and perhaps even radical change if taken seriously and implemented. Churches should use the Rio Declaration to press for changes in their own societies and internationally. Churches should also be prepared to participate in further movement towards a full Earth Charter, perhaps in 1995, the 50th anniversary of the UN.

b) Biodiversity

The richness and variety of life forms on earth bear witness to God's creativity. We acknowledge that the traditional anthropocentric nature of Christian theology has contributed to one species, human beings, destroying and threatening many other life forms. Furthermore, the powerful within the human community are seeking to gain ownership rights over life forms to extract maximum economic profit.

The international community must take action to protect biodiversity. The Biodiversity Convention signed by 153 nations at Rio is a first step, but further action to limit the destructive impact of societies generally, and transnational corporations and governments specifically, is urgently required. Churches can play an important role by advocating principles that:

— respect the inherent integrity of all species (cf. the Rights of Nature produced by the World Alliance of Reformed Churches);
— conserve biodiversity in order to stabilize the life-support system of the planet, enable sustainable development, and ensure equitable access to generative resources;
— protect the territorial rights of indigenous peoples on whose lands great varieties of life exist;
— control the life-threatening transboundary movement of hazardous wastes and their disposal (cf. Basel Convention 1989) as well as their destructive impacts within countries.

c) Climate change

The WCC and many member churches have been deeply concerned about global warming. They see it as a threat to creation caused largely by the polluting emissions of industrialized nations but with the adverse consequences experienced most severely by developing countries. The climate convention signed at UNCED is a first step to address the problem but falls far short of what is needed. Largely because of opposition from the United States, the convention contains no specific targets or schedules for limiting greenhouse gas emissions.

Reducing the threat of global warming clearly implies the need within industrialized countries for a drastic change in life-styles, a major reduction in energy consumption, and a significant reorientation in their economies. Scientific evidence indicates the need for a global reduction of carbon dioxide emissions by 2 per cent annually if ecosystems are not to be irrevocably damaged. In order to allow for the development needs of the South, a higher rate (e.g. 3 per cent) should be required for industrialized countries. Churches should encourage their societies, through whatever means possible, to pursue such targets as well as limiting other greenhouse gas emissions, banning CFCs, drastically increasing energy conservation and efficiency. Nuclear energy is not an appropriate alternative to fossil fuels either from an ecological or economic perspective. Reducing energy demand is the better approach. All countries, both in the North and in the South, should promote the growth of forests and other plant life as a carbon sink (cf. Seoul JPIC statement, Gwatt consultation report, "Churches on Climate Change").

As southern countries pursue development, global warming challenges them not to repeat the mistakes of the North. Limiting the increase in their emissions is complicated by many economic factors including the link between poverty and deforestation. International cooperation and significant transfers of financial resources and technology will be required if the south is to pursue sustainable and just development models. Cancellation of crushing foreign debts would help the move to ecologically-sustainable economies in the South.

Churches around the world should bear witness to the significant life-style changes that will be required at the local level to minimize global warming and should support international negotiations for stronger treaties on climate change at the global level.

d) Forests

Forests, both southern tropical/subtropical and northern boreal ones, are key to the survival and health of the earth and its inhabitants including trees' important role in limiting global warming through acting as carbon sinks. Churches view the present forestry practices in many countries, both industrialized and developing ones, as clearly unsustainable. In many places, these practices also threaten the cultures and survival of indigenous forest peoples who depend upon these forests and who have lived for generations in harmony with them. Countries were not able to agree on a forestry convention for signing at UNCED. Instead, various nations supported a more limited Declaration of Principles ón Forestry Management.

Recognizing that forestry, like other issues, raises complex problems of national sovereignty, nonetheless, churches should encourage actions nationally and internationally that:
— ensure the long-term sustainability of the earth's forests;
— recognize and respect the territorial rights of indigenous forest peoples and draw on their wisdom in caring for the forests;
— give priority to halting the loss of primary forests and forest ecosystems;
— oppose unsustainable forestry practices of their national corporations whether operating in their own country or another;
— support in solidarity those who are resisting the destruction of forests.

e) Agenda 21

The ambitious work plan in many areas of environment and development agreed to by UNCED in the document titled Agenda 21 will provide challenges for all countries well into the next century. Significant issues, including the funding for Agenda 21 proposals, remain unresolved. Churches must play an ongoing role monitoring these international negotiations and encouraging their countries to participate actively and constructively towards resolving the critical problems of environment and development.

Theology

This is one of the group reports prepared at the WCC meeting. These reports were "received" by the meeting for further study and action.

The World Council of Churches ecumenical gathering, with the theme "Searching for the New Heavens and the New Earth", met in Rio de Janeiro in June 1992.

Gathering at a critical time in the history of the whole earth, Christians recognized the need to develop new theological understanding and interpretation of the biblical tradition.

Creation

We believe in God the Creator, the Source of Life: "The Lord, who created the heavens and stretched them out, who spread the earth and what comes from it" (Isaiah 42:5a, NRSV).

We recognize that people from different cultures and religions, especially the indigenous peoples, have their own stories of the origin of the universe, and we have to be in dialogue with one another as co-inhabitants of the planet.

We affirm the goodness of God's creation and the intrinsic worth of all beings. Anthropocentric, hierarchical and patriarchal understandings of creation leads to the alienation of human beings from each other, from nature, and from God. The current ecological crisis calls us to move towards an eco-centred theology of creation which emphasizes God's Spirit in creation (Genesis 1:2, Ps. 104), and human beings as an integral part of nature. Instead of dominating nature, men and women have the responsibility to preserve, cultivate the earth, and to work with God for the sustainability of the planet. Without a just and equitable distribution of resources and the liberation of people from all forms of bondage, we cannot celebrate together the gracious love of the Creator and the goodness of creation.

Anthropology

From the scientists we learn that human beings came into existence much later than the plants and other living organisms. With diverse cultures and languages, people of all races belong to one single species.

An eco-centred theology of creation requires us to re-examine some of the basic presuppositions of theological anthropology. A hierarchical understanding of imago Dei, putting human beings infinitely above all creation, must be replaced by a more relational view. Human beings are created for the purpose of communion with God and all the living and non-living things. In the example of Jesus, we see a life-style characterized by simplicity, humility and openness to nature. Responding to the love of God, human beings must act as moral agents, guided by an ethic of care and responsibility.

The doctrine of sin must be interpreted in a new way in the light of the ecological crisis. We are increasingly aware of the different dimensions of sin: personal, spiritual, social and global. The addictions of human beings to power and to the accumulation of wealth both degrades the earth and undermines the lives of generations to come. A narrow understanding of property creates an ownership system which impedes the just distribution of material goods and the sharing of fruits of sciences and the new biotechnology.

It is as though the earth itself bears the scars of human sinfulness (Isaiah 49:19). We are impelled to repent of our destruction of the earth and we are called to conversion. We have to listen to the earth's groanings in travail (Romans 8), to develop a new sensitivity, and to act in solidarity with those struggling for the fullness of life.

Eschatology

We believe that the earth as it is no longer reflects justice and peace, and the glory of God. Living under the apocalyptic judgment of God, we remember the vision of "a new heaven and a new earth", emerged out of the historical crisis of the Hebrew people.

As Christians, we live in faith and hope. Hope is not passive waiting, but active expectation. We believe that in Jesus Christ all things hold together and are reconciled to God (Colossians 1:17-20). Christians have to participate in the healing and reconciling process, creating visible signs for the new heaven and the new earth.

We believe that the unity of the churches is important for our common witness, so that the Christian community may be an agent and a sign of the integrity of creation. The Holy Spirit, working through us and in us, empowers us to resist evil, and renews our faith and hope.

Spirituality

We believe that the Spirit of God is moving to transform both the church and the world. There is a new awareness to proclaim a sustainable spirituality characterized by a simple life-style that preserves the earth and seeks justice. It is a spirituality of listening to the poor and to the indigenous peoples. It is a spirituality of resistance to all forms of oppression of living things and the earth. It is a spirituality that delights in and works for the forgiveness of debts and for the year of Jubilee.

We recommend that the churches:

1. Re-read the Bible and reinterpret our traditions in light of the ecological crisis.
2. Raise the ecological sensitivity of church members through preaching, teaching, performing rituals, and adopting simplicity of life-style.
3. Express solidarity with children, the poor, women, and people torn by war and poverty as concrete commitments to the JPIC process.
4. Develop and teach a new understanding of the theology of creation in theological education and in ministerial formation.

One Earth Community

Preamble

We, representatives of religious communities from around the world, have gathered together to respond to the challenge presented by the United Nations Conference on Environment and Development. Representing major religious traditions and diverse cultures and regions, as well as groups working in local situations on issues of environment and development, we have sought to discover how our various concerns bring moral, ethical and spiritual perspectives to the agenda for UNCED. In particular, we have considered various proposals for the Earth Charter from the standpoints of our shared convictions about the unity of the human family and the oneness of the earth and the particular beliefs of our various religious traditions. We offer the following declaration and statement of principles as an expression of our work and commitment.

Life is a gift and elicits our respect, awe and reverence. We are one earth community, one human family, and we share one destiny. We cherish and respect the rich diversity of life, and celebrate the beauty of the earth. For us, as members of one family, love and caring are the basis of our relationship with one another and with nature. The earth community is our greatest gift and sacred trust. We recognize a call to receive this gift gratefully, to draw earth's sustenance carefully, and to share it equitably.

The threat

This vision has been distorted. Now the life of the earth community is threatened with destruction. In the name of human progress and development, there is growing devastation of nature and widespread and increasing poverty. The present world economy makes the rich richer and the poor poorer. It has promoted consumerism and greed and a preoccupation of people and nations with money, control and power at the cost of justice and cultural and spiritual enhancement. Rising international debt enslaves some peoples, even as it enriches others.

The streams and seas which give life are used as dumps for our wastes, the forests which give life are destroyed for crass commercial gain, the soil which gives life is squandered for profit to benefit the few. We have become alienated from ourselves, from one another and from nature. The dominant pattern of development has led to the degradation of cultures, the destruction of nature and the death of millions of our brothers and sisters and threatens future generations. It has intensified the exploitation of women and children and has further marginalized indigenous peoples. Although it has given short-term benefits to a substantial minority, for most it has given agony.

The way forward

We are at a major turning point in which we can either continue along the path of self-destruction or turn towards restoration and renewal. The human family, in which the unique quality of all its members is recognized and protected, must bring itself back into harmony with nature and the universe. We need to listen to those communities which have remained close to the earth, and recognize and incorporate the wisdom culled from women's traditional links with nature. We have to realize that there are limits to growth and that the idea of an ever-expanding economy contradicts the capacities of the earth community. We must end the over-consumption of industrialized societies. We must make institutions accountable to the people whose lives they touch. We must restructure economic institutions to make them serve the needs of the poor and function in harmony with ecological reality. We see every member of the family as a full participant, sharing equally in the gifts of nature, the work to be done and the fruits of that work. We need to reaffirm the importance of justice, frugality, humility and reverence for life and nature.

Considerations for an Earth Charter

The Earth Charter should recognize that our unjust exploitation and destruction of the environment, as well as our reverence for it and our conservation of it, have spiritual and ethical dimensions which undergird the following principles.

Principles

These in part make reference to UN document PC/78.

1. *Responsibility towards the earth as a whole:* The earth, with its diverse life forms, is a functioning whole. Whatever we

humans do to the web of life we do to ourselves. States and individuals have the obligation to respect the functioning of the whole. Rights and obligations of both states and individuals need to be defined within this perspective.

2. *The indivisibility of ecological justice and social justice:* We affirm the indivisibility of justice to the environment and social justice. The Earth Charter must clearly recognize that environmental destruction and injustice have systemic causes such as the dominant development model itself with its emphasis on capital intensive industrialization. The main victims of this approach to development are the nations and peoples of the South. As recent studies and common experience have shown, women and children bear a particularly heavy share of the burdens of poverty and economic degradation. We must acknowledge the need for limits to growth and a just sharing of resources in the interests of sustainable sufficiency for all. The development of environmentally safe technology, rooted in the needs and experiences of the people who benefit from it, becomes important in this context. Technologies already in the hands of women and traditional communities must not be overlooked.

3. *Access to education:* In addition to encouraging educators to include the environment as a subject of study, the Earth Charter should reaffirm the importance of universal access to education and the need for education to include the development of the whole person. The central role of women as educators and carriers of information and culture should be recognized. Moreover, the open access of people to information and communication on all issues including the environment should be recognized as an essential right. Education should cultivate personal responsibility and inclusive concern for humanity and the earth.

4. *The rights of future generations:* Future as well as present generations of all peoples have a right to existence and to their share in the goods of the earth. This right places further responsibilities and limits on the way in which resources ought to be used in the present. These rights need to be incorporated in legislation and internationally binding agreements.

5. *Participation of individuals and groups in decision-making:* All persons should have the opportunity to participate, individually and with others, in the formulation and implemen-

tation of decisions affecting their environment. Governments and institutions must be accountable to their people. This opportunity is particularly important for groups such as women, indigenous peoples, children and the poor who are particularly vulnerable to the impact of environmental degradation and who are often excluded from participation in decision-making. The expertise of women as environmental managers must be recognized.

6. *Establishing procedures and mechanisms permitting a transnational approach to environmental issues and disputes:* Since the environmental crisis has global dimensions there is an urgent need for increased mutual accountability of the nations in this field. As religious people we support procedures and mechanisms for avoiding environmental harm and for settling disputes among nations on environmental issues and for holding states accountable for their actions. Increasingly internationally accepted standards of environmental performance need to be developed. In order to enforce such standards the creation of an international court or other mechanisms to deal with environmental issues should be envisaged.

7. *Principle of precautionary/preventive action:* The burden of proof for the safety of activities which may potentially damage the environment should increasingly fall on the promoters of such activities. Decisions should be based upon adequate environmental, social and cultural impact assessments. The emphasis should be shifted from confidence in technological solutions to environmental damage to prevention.

8. *Affirming the "polluter pays" principle as an international standard:* The cost of environmental damage, created by technological and industrial activities, is to be borne by those who cause it. The "polluter pays" principle needs to be affirmed. In particular, industrialized nations should be held responsible for the degradation which they cause.

9. *Protection of biodiversity:* The world religious community respects the diversity of species and calls for its protection. We are concerned about the extent to which the international patenting of biological life forms has led to the exploitation of the genetic resources of the South. We are also concerned about the disappearance of local food crops and medicinal plants. We have a basic responsibility to ensure that all forms of life are

respected and preserved. An Earth Charter should address this problem.

10. *Wealth, poverty and the peoples of the world:* The Earth Charter should address the question of the carrying capacity of the earth by dealing with factors linked to population growth, the unjust distribution of resources and the relationship between the consumption of resources of the rich and the poverty of the poor. Continuing efforts need to be made to develop new social, economic and cultural indicators of wealth and poverty.

11. *The impact of militarization on environment and development:* Although the proliferation of nuclear weapons and other weapons of mass destruction poses the gravest most immediate and long-term threat, other forms of military activity including the arms trade and the transfer of military technology are also significant. War is ecologically disruptive in a number of ways. It always results in widespread, temporary and permanent destruction of both the human and physical environment, including dramatically increased consumption and destruction of natural resources. The forced migration of peoples and establishment of refugee camps can also have a significant impact on the environment well beyond the war-torn region. Conflicts must be resolved through peaceful means. Disarmament must be a priority for any action programme.

12. *Fundamental change in life-styles required:* There is a need to break the addiction to life-styles based on possession and high consumption patterns. There is also an urgent need for the North to drastically reduce its levels of consumption and waste.

Rio Declaration on Environment and Development

The United Nations Conference on Environment and Development,
- Having met at Rio de Janeiro from 3 to 14 June 1992,
- Reaffirming the Declaration of the United Nations Conference on the Human Environment, adopted at Stockholm on 16 June 1972, and seeking to build upon it,
- With the goal of establishing a new and equitable global partnership through the creation of new levels of cooperation among states, key sectors of societies and people,
- Working towards international agreements which respect the interests of all and protect the integrity of the global environmental and developmental system,
- Recognizing the integral and interdependent nature of the Earth, our home,

Proclaims that:

Principle 1: Human beings are at the centre of concerns for sustainable development. They are entitled to a healthy and productive life in harmony with nature.

Principle 2: States have, in accordance with the Charter of the United Nations and the principles of international law, the sovereign right to exploit their own resources pursuant to their own environmental and developmental policies, and the responsibility to ensure that activities within their jurisdiction or control do not cause damage to the environment of other states or of areas beyond the limits of national jurisdiction.

Principle 3: The right to development must be fulfilled so as to equitably meet developmental and environmental needs of present and future generations.

Principle 4: In order to achieve sustainable development, environmental protection shall constitute an integral part of the development process and cannot be considered in isolation from it.

Principle 5: All states and all people shall cooperate in the essential task of eradicating poverty as an indispensable requirement for sustainable development, in order to decrease the disparities in standards of living and better meet the needs of the majority of the people of the world.

Principle 6: The special situation and needs of developing countries, particularly the least developed and those most environmentally vulnerable, shall be given special priority. International actions in the field of environment and development should also address the interests and needs of all countries.

Principle 7: States shall cooperate in a spirit of global partnership to conserve, protect and restore the health and integrity of the earth's ecosystem. In view of the different contributions to global environmental degradation, states have common but differentiated responsibilities. The developed countries acknowledge the responsibility that they bear in the international pursuit of sustainable development in view of the pressures their societies place on the global environment and of the technologies and financial resources they command.

Principle 8: To achieve sustainable development and a high quality of life for all people, states should reduce and eliminate unsustainable patterns of production and consumption and promote appropriate demographic policies.

Principle 9: States should cooperate to strengthen endogenous capacity-building for sustainable development by improving scientific understanding through exchanges of scientific and technological knowledge, and by enhancing the development, adaptation, diffusion and transfer of technologies, including new and innovative technologies.

Principle 10: Environmental issues are best handled with the participation of all concerned citizens, at the relevant level. At the national level, each individual shall have appropriate access to information concerning the environment that is held by public authorities, including information on hazardous materials and activities in their communities, and the opportunity to participate in decision-making processes. States shall facilitate and encourage public awareness and participation by making information widely available. Effective access to judicial and administrative proceedings, including redress and remedy, shall be provided.

Principle 11: States shall enact effective environmental legislation. Environmental standards, management objectives and priorities should reflect the environmental and development context to which they apply. Standards applied by some countries may be inappropriate and of unwarranted economic and social cost to other countries, in particular developing countries.

Principle 12: States should cooperate to promote a supportive and open international economic system that would lead to economic growth and sustainable development in all countries, to better address the problems of environmental degradation. Trade policy measures for environmental purposes should not constitute a means of arbitrary or unjustifiable discrimination or a disguised restriction on international trade. Unilateral actions to deal with environmental challenges outside the jurisdiction of the importing country should be avoided. Environmental measures addressing transboundary or global environmental problems should, as far as possible, be based on an international consensus.

Principle 13: States shall develop national law regarding liability and compensation for the victims of pollution and other environmental damage. States shall also cooperate in an expeditious and more determined manner to develop further international law regarding liability and compensation for adverse effects of environmental damage caused by activities within their jurisdiction or control to areas beyond their jurisdiction.

Principle 14: States should effectively cooperate to discourage or prevent the relocation and transfer to other states of any activities and substances that cause severe environmental degradation or are found to be harmful to human health.

Principle 15: In order to protect the environment, the precautionary approach shall be widely applied by states according to their capabilities. Where there are threats of serious or irreversible damage, lack of full scientific certainty shall not be used as a reason for postponing cost-effective measures to prevent environmental degradation.

Principle 16: National authorities should endeavour to promote the internalization of environmental costs and the use of economic instruments, taking into account the approach that the polluter should, in principle, bear the cost of pollution, with due regard to the public interest and without distorting international trade and investment.

Principle 17: Environmental impact assessment, as a national instrument, shall be undertaken for proposed activities that are likely to have a significant adverse impact on the environment and are subject to a decision of a competent national authority.

Principle 18: States shall immediately notify other states of any natural disasters or other emergencies that are likely to produce sudden harmful effects on the environment of those states. Every effort shall be made by the international community to help states so afflicted.

Principle 19: States shall provide prior and timely notification and relevant information to potentially affected states on activities that may have a significant adverse transboundary environmental effect and shall consult with those states at an early stage and in good faith.

Principle 20: Women have a vital role in environmental management and development. Their full participation is therefore essential to achieve sustainable development.

Principle 21: The creativity, ideals and courage of the youth of the world should be mobilized to forge a global partnership in order to achieve sustainable development and ensure a better future for all.

Principle 22: Indigenous people and their communities, and other local communities, have a vital role in environmental management and development because of their knowledge and traditional practices. States should recognize and duly support their identity, culture and interests and enable their effective participation in the achievement of sustainable development.

Principle 23: The environment and natural resources of people under oppression, domination and occupation shall be protected.

Principle 24: Warfare is inherently destructive of sustainable development. States shall therefore respect international law providing protection for the environment in times of armed conflict and cooperate in its further development, as necessary.

Principle 25: Peace, development and environmental protection are interdependent and indivisible.

Principle 26: States shall resolve all their environmental disputes peacefully and by appropriate means in accordance with the Charter of the United Nations.

Principle 27: States and people shall cooperate in good faith and in a spirit of partnership in the fulfilment of the principles embodied in this declaration and in the further development of international law in the field of sustainable development.